QUEBEC TRAVEL GUIDE 2024

A New Updated Companion to Exploring Top Attractions, Hidden Gems, and Must-See Sites for Families, Couples, Solo Travelers, and Foodies in The Beautiful Province

Albert N. Allred

Disclaimer

We've put together the "**Quebec Travel Guide 2024**" with great care to provide you with the latest and most accurate information about this beautiful province. However, please keep in mind that details such as **prices, operating hours, tour availability, and weather conditions** can change quickly in Quebec.

To ensure your trip goes smoothly and is as enjoyable as possible, we recommend double-checking these details with **hotels, tour operators, transportation services, and official sources** before you set out on your Quebec adventure. Although we strive to give you the best and most current information, verifying these details on your own will help you avoid surprises and make the most of your visit to this charming province.

Contents

Welcome to The Beautiful Province
Northwest Territories
Ivujivik
Baffin Island
Hudson Bay
Quaqtaq
Kangiqsuk
Povungnituk
Ungava Bay
Labrador Sea
Inukjuak
Kuujjuaq
Sanikiluaq
Belcher Islands
Lake l'Eau Claire
0 150 mi
Lake Bienville
Schefferville
LABRADOR
QUEBEC
Labrador City
Lake Mistassini
Gagnon
Sept-Iles
Havre St Pierre
La Sarre
Chibougamau
Ile D' Anticosti
Amos
Jonquiére
Gulf of St. Lawrence
Val d'Or
Chicoutimi
NEW BRUNSWICK
Quebec
PRINCE EDWARD IS
Trois-Rivieres
Montreal
Ottawa
Sherbrooke
NOVA SCOTIA
Atlantic Ocean
ONTARIO
U. S. A.

Introduction

Quebec City stole my heart the minute I stepped off the plane this year. It was my first time visiting, and let me tell you, it was pure magic. The city has this old-world charm that just pulls you in. The cobblestone streets, the cute little shops, the smell of fresh croissants... It's like stepping into a fairytale.

One of my favorite things to do was just wander around Old Quebec. It's like a maze of narrow alleyways, each one more charming than the last. You'll stumble upon hidden courtyards, adorable cafes, and shops selling unique crafts. I got lost a few times, but that's part of the fun!

If you're a history buff, you'll love the Plains of Abraham. It's a big park where a famous battle took place, but now it's a peaceful place to relax and enjoy the views. The Château Frontenac is another must-see. It's this grand hotel perched on a hill overlooking the city, and it's absolutely stunning.

One night, I had dinner at a traditional sugar shack. It was such a fun experience! They serve all sorts of maple syrup treats, and everyone sits at long tables, so you get to chat with the locals and other travelers. It was like a big family dinner.

Of course, no trip to Quebec would be complete without trying poutine. It's a Canadian classic – fries covered in cheese curds and gravy. It might sound weird, but trust me, it's delicious! I also had some amazing croissants and pastries – the bakeries in Quebec are out of this world.

I could go on and on about Quebec, but I don't want to spoil the surprise. Just know that it's a city that will capture your heart. The people are warm and friendly, the food is incredible, and the scenery is breathtaking. Whether you're exploring the historic sites, enjoying the local cuisine, or just soaking up the atmosphere, you're guaranteed to have an unforgettable time.

So, if you're looking for a travel destination that's a little bit different, a little bit magical, and a whole lot of fun, put Quebec City at the top of your list. You won't regret it!

Chapter 1: Discovering The Beautiful Province(Quebec)

A. Overview of Quebec

Welcome to Quebec, a province that seamlessly blends history, culture, and stunning natural beauty. Quebec is the largest province in Canada by area and the second largest by population, making it a diverse and exciting destination for travelers.

Quebec's story begins with its founding by French explorer Samuel de Champlain in 1608. Quebec City, the capital of the province, is one of the oldest cities in North America. As you walk through the streets of Old Quebec, you'll feel like you've stepped back in time. This area is a UNESCO World Heritage Site, renowned for its well-preserved colonial architecture, cobblestone streets, and the iconic Château Frontenac, a grand hotel that dominates the skyline.

The province's French heritage is a defining characteristic. French is the official language, and the culture is steeped in French traditions. This influence is most evident in Montreal, Quebec's largest city, known for its vibrant arts scene, diverse culinary offerings, and bustling festivals. Montreal is a city where historic charm meets modern flair, offering something for everyone.

Quebec is a province that offers a wide range of experiences. From the urban excitement of Montreal to the historic allure of Quebec City, there is much to see and do. The province is known for its stunning natural landscapes, including the Laurentian Mountains and the Gaspé Peninsula. These areas provide endless opportunities for outdoor activities such as hiking, skiing, and kayaking.

The St. Lawrence River is another central feature of Quebec's geography. It runs through the heart of the province, offering scenic views and numerous recreational opportunities.

Whale watching along the river is a popular activity, providing a chance to see these majestic creatures up close.

Quebec's culture is vibrant and diverse. The province is home to a variety of festivals throughout the year, celebrating everything from music and film to food and winter sports. The Quebec Winter Carnival, held in Quebec City, is one of the largest and most famous winter festivals in the world, drawing visitors from all over to enjoy its ice sculptures, parades, and outdoor activities.

No visit to Quebec is complete without sampling its unique cuisine. The province is famous for dishes such as poutine, a hearty combination of fries, cheese curds, and gravy, and tourtière, a savory meat pie. Quebec is also a major producer of maple syrup, and visiting a sugar shack to see how this sweet treat is made is a must-do activity.

In Montreal, the food scene is diverse and exciting. From high-end restaurants to cozy cafes, there is something to suit every taste. The city is known for its bagels, smoked meat sandwiches, and diverse international cuisine, reflecting its multicultural population.

Quebec is a year-round destination, offering something special in every season. Winter transforms the province into a snowy wonderland, perfect for skiing, snowboarding, and ice skating. Spring brings blooming flowers and a sense of renewal, while summer is the season for festivals, outdoor concerts, and exploring the great outdoors. In the fall, the province's forests burst into vibrant colors, providing a stunning backdrop for hiking and sightseeing.

Whether you're a history buff, a nature lover, a foodie, or an adventure seeker, Quebec has something to offer. Its unique blend of old-world charm and modern vibrancy makes it a destination like no other. So pack your bags and get ready to explore all that Quebec has to offer. Enjoy your journey!

B. History and Culture

Welcome to Quebec, a province rich in history and culture. As you explore Quebec, you'll encounter stories that span centuries, from the ancient times of Indigenous peoples to the vibrant, multicultural society it is today.

Indigenous Roots

Quebec's history begins long before European settlers arrived. Indigenous peoples, such as the Iroquois and Algonquin, have lived in the region for thousands of years. Their cultures and traditions are integral to Quebec's heritage. You can learn about their history and contributions at various cultural centers and museums throughout the province.

French Exploration and Settlement

The European chapter of Quebec's history started in 1534 when French explorer Jacques Cartier claimed the land for France. However, it wasn't until 1608 that Samuel de Champlain founded Quebec City, marking the beginning of New France. This colony quickly became a center for the fur trade and expanded with settlements like Montreal and Trois-Rivières.

British Conquest and the Quebec Act

Quebec's strategic importance led to fierce battles between the French and British. In 1759, the British defeated the French at the Battle of the Plains of Abraham, bringing New France under British control. Despite this change, the French language and culture remained strong due to the Quebec Act of 1774, which allowed French Canadians to retain their language, laws, and Catholic religion. This act was pivotal in maintaining Quebec's unique identity within the British Empire.

The Quiet Revolution and Modern Quebec

The 1960s brought significant social and political changes to Quebec, known as the Quiet Revolution. This period led to the secularization of society, modernization of the economy, and a rise in Quebec nationalism. The movement fostered a strong sense of identity and pride among Quebecers, resulting in two referendums on Quebec sovereignty in 1980 and 1995, both of which resulted in votes to remain within Canada.

Cultural Vibrancy

Today, Quebec is celebrated for its vibrant culture, which is a blend of its French heritage and diverse immigrant influences. The province is predominantly French-speaking, but in cities like Montreal, you'll find a cosmopolitan mix of languages and cultures. Montreal, known for its dynamic arts scene, hosts numerous festivals, concerts, and culinary events, making it a cultural hotspot.

Exploring Quebec's Cultural Heritage

Quebec's history is reflected in its many attractions. Visit the Citadelle of Quebec and the Plains of Abraham to understand the military history that shaped the province. Explore museums like the Musée de la Civilisation and the Musée national des beaux-arts du Québec, which offer insights into the province's past and present. Don't miss the stunning architecture of historic churches such as the Notre-Dame de Québec Basilica-Cathedral.

C. Lesser Known Facts You Should Know About Quebec

When visiting Quebec, you're sure to encounter the well-known highlights like the historic streets of Old Quebec, the bustling cultural hub of Montreal, and the stunning natural beauty of the Laurentian Mountains. However, Quebec holds many lesser-known facts that can enrich your understanding and appreciation of this unique province. Here are some fascinating tidbits that might surprise you:

1. Old Quebec: A Living Museum
Old Quebec is not only a UNESCO World Heritage Site but also one of the few remaining fortified city areas north of Mexico. Walking through its cobblestone streets is like stepping back in time. The walls that surround the city have protected it for centuries and are still intact today, providing a living glimpse into the past.

2. Île d'Orléans: The Cradle of French America**
Just a short drive from Quebec City, Île d'Orléans is often called the "Cradle of French America" because it's one of the first areas in Quebec settled by the French. The island is dotted with centuries-old homes and churches, and it's a great place to taste local products like cider, cheese, and chocolates.

3. Maple Syrup Capital
Quebec is the world's largest producer of maple syrup, responsible for more than 70% of the global supply. Visiting a "cabane à sucre" (sugar shack) during the spring maple season is a quintessential Quebec experience, where you can see the syrup-making process and enjoy traditional meals.

4. Montmorency Falls: Taller Than Niagara

Montmorency Falls, located just outside Quebec City, is 83 meters high—about 30 meters taller than Niagara Falls. The falls can be explored by foot, via a cable car, or for the adventurous, by zipline.

5. The Huron-Wendat Nation

The Huron-Wendat Nation, near Quebec City, offers visitors an immersive experience in Indigenous culture. The traditional Huron site at Wendake includes a recreated village, guided tours, and cultural demonstrations, allowing a deep dive into the history and traditions of the Huron-Wendat people.

6. Underground City in Montreal

Montreal features an extensive underground city known as "RÉSO" (La Ville Souterraine). Spanning over 33 kilometers, this network of tunnels connects shopping centers, hotels, and metro stations, offering a convenient and weather-proof way to navigate the city.

7. Distinct Seasons

Quebec experiences four distinct seasons, each offering its unique charm. The province is a winter wonderland perfect for skiing and snowboarding, blossoms in spring with beautiful flowers, hosts numerous festivals in summer, and showcases spectacular fall foliage.

8. Bilingualism

While French is the official language of Quebec, English is widely spoken, especially in Montreal. This bilingual nature makes Quebec an accessible destination for English-speaking tourists while also providing an authentic French cultural experience.

9. Gastronomic Delights

Quebec's culinary scene is a delightful mix of French and local influences. Must-try dishes include poutine (fries topped with cheese curds and gravy), tourtière (a traditional meat pie), and artisanal cheeses. The province also boasts a vibrant food truck culture and numerous high-end restaurants.

10. Cultural Festivals

Quebec is known for its vibrant festival scene. The Quebec Winter Carnival is one of the largest and most famous winter festivals in the world, featuring ice sculptures, parades, and outdoor activities. Montreal hosts the Montreal

Jazz Festival, attracting artists and visitors from around the globe.

Chapter 2: Planning Your Trip

A. Best Times to Visit

Spring (March to May)

Spring in Quebec is a wonderful time to visit if you enjoy mild weather and blooming landscapes. As the snow melts, the province awakens with flowers and greenery. It's an excellent season for exploring parks, enjoying outdoor activities, and visiting sugar shacks where you can experience traditional maple syrup production. While the weather can be unpredictable, with temperatures ranging from 35°F to 64°F, it's a refreshing and quieter time to explore.

Summer (June to August)

Summer is the most popular time to visit Quebec, thanks to warm temperatures and a lively festival scene. With highs around 77°F and plenty of sunshine, it’s perfect for outdoor dining, exploring historic sites, and enjoying numerous festivals like the Festival d'été de Québec and the Montreal Jazz Festival. This is also the best time for hiking, river surfing in Montreal, and enjoying the vibrant street life.

Fall (September to November)

Fall is a spectacular season to visit Quebec, especially if you love stunning fall foliage. The temperatures are cooler, ranging from 36°F to 64°F, making it ideal for hiking, leaf-peeping, and enjoying harvest festivals. The crowds thin out after Labor Day, providing a more relaxed atmosphere. It's a great time to visit local markets and enjoy seasonal dishes featuring fresh produce.

Winter (December to February)

Winter in Quebec is a magical time, transforming the province into a snowy wonderland. With temperatures often dipping below 0°F, it's the perfect season for winter sports like skiing, snowboarding, ice skating, and snowshoeing. The Quebec Winter Carnival, one of the world's largest winter festivals, takes place during this time and features ice sculptures, parades, and the famous Bonhomme Carnaval mascot. The snowy landscapes make it a picturesque time for visiting historic sites and enjoying cozy indoor activities.

B. Travel Requirements and Visas

Planning your trip to Quebec involves understanding the necessary travel requirements and visa regulations. Here's a practical guide to help you navigate these essential steps smoothly.

Travel Documents

1. Passport: Ensure your passport is valid for the duration of your stay. For most international visitors, a passport is required to enter Canada, including Quebec.

2. Electronic Travel Authorization (eTA): Travelers from visa-exempt countries, except for U.S. citizens, need an eTA to fly to or transit through a Canadian airport. The eTA is electronically linked to your passport and is valid for up to five years or until your passport expires. You can apply for an eTA online, and it usually takes just a few minutes to get approval.

3. Visa Requirements:

- **U.S. Citizens:** Do not require a visa for visits of up to six months but must carry a valid passport.
- **Other Nationals:** Depending on your nationality, you may need a visa. Check the Government of Canada's official website for the most current visa requirements and to apply if necessary.

Special Considerations

1. COVID-19 Regulations: As of 2024, there are no COVID-19 restrictions for entering Quebec. However, it's always best to check the latest health advisories and travel updates before your trip.

2. Quebec-specific Immigration: Quebec has its own immigration process separate from the rest of Canada. If you're planning to move to Quebec, you'll need to apply for a Certificat de sélection du Québec (CSQ) before applying for permanent residency through the federal government.

Practical Tips

1. Advance Declaration: Use the Advance Declaration feature in the ArriveCAN app to submit your customs and immigration declaration before flying into Canada. This can save you time at the border.

2. Customs: Familiarize yourself with what you can bring into Canada. Certain items like fresh produce, meats, and dairy products may have restrictions. Check the Canada Border Services Agency (CBSA) website for detailed information on customs regulations.

3. International Experience Canada (IEC): If you're between 18 to 35 years old, you can take advantage of the IEC program to work and travel in Canada. This program allows you to gain valuable international work experience and explore Canada for up to two years.

C. Budgeting for Your Trip

Planning a trip to Quebec involves not only deciding where to go and what to see but also how to manage your expenses. Here's a practical guide to help you budget for your Quebec adventure, ensuring you get the most out of your trip without breaking the bank.

Accommodation

Hotels and Hostels:

- **Hotels:** Quebec offers a wide range of hotels from budget to luxury. In major cities like Montreal and Quebec City, budget hotels start at around CAD 100 per night, while mid-range options are around CAD 150-250. Luxury hotels and historic inns, such as the Fairmont Le Château Frontenac, can cost upwards of CAD 300 per night.
- **Hostels:** For budget travelers, hostels are a great option, with prices ranging from CAD 30-50 per night for a dorm bed. Private rooms in hostels are also available at higher rates.

Vacation Rentals:

- **Airbnb and Vacation Rentals:** Renting an apartment or a house can be a cost-effective option, especially for families or groups. Prices vary widely depending on the location and season, but you can find entire apartments starting at CAD 100 per night.

Food and Dining

Dining Out:

- **Budget Meals:** Fast food and casual dining options like poutine shops, cafes, and food trucks cost around CAD 10-20 per meal.
- **Mid-Range:** Dining at mid-range restaurants typically cost between CAD 25-50 per person. Quebec's culinary scene includes a variety of international cuisines, so you'll have plenty of choices.
- **High-End:** For fine dining, expect to spend upwards of CAD 75 per person. Quebec is known for its French-inspired cuisine, and cities like Montreal boast numerous gourmet restaurants.

Groceries:

- If you prefer cooking your meals, groceries for a week can cost around CAD 60-100 per person, depending on your preferences and dietary needs.

Transportation

Public Transport:

- **Cities:** Montreal and Quebec City have efficient public transportation systems. A single ride on the Montreal Metro costs CAD 3.50, and a day pass is around CAD 10. In Quebec City, a single bus ticket is CAD 3.75, and day passes are available for CAD 8.60.

- **Intercity Travel:** Buses and trains connect major cities in Quebec. A bus ride from Montreal to Quebec City costs around CAD 40-60 one way. VIA Rail offers train services, with prices varying based on the class and time of booking.

Car Rentals:

- Renting a car can be convenient for exploring more remote areas. Rental costs start at around CAD 40-60 per day for a standard vehicle, excluding fuel and insurance. Remember to factor in the cost of parking, especially in urban areas.

Activities and Attractions

Free and Low-Cost Activities:

- Many of Quebec's attractions, such as parks, historical sites, and festivals, are free or have minimal entrance fees. Walking tours, hiking in national parks, and visiting local markets are great ways to experience Quebec on a budget.

Paid Attractions:

- Entry fees for museums and historical sites typically range from CAD 10-20. For example, admission to the Musée de la Civilisation in Quebec City is CAD 17.50 for adults. Ski resorts, amusement parks, and guided tours will cost more, so plan these activities based on your interests and budget.

Miscellaneous Costs

Travel Insurance:

- It's wise to have travel insurance to cover unexpected medical expenses, trip cancellations, or lost belongings. Basic travel insurance can cost around CAD 20-50 per week, depending on the coverage.

Souvenirs and Shopping:

- Budget a reasonable amount for souvenirs and shopping, depending on your preferences. Local crafts, maple syrup products, and clothing are popular items.

Chapter 3: Getting to Quebec

A. Air Travel

When flying to Quebec, you'll primarily be arriving at one of the major airports in the province. Each airport offers unique amenities and services to ensure a smooth travel experience.

Major Airports in Quebec

1. Montreal-Pierre Elliott Trudeau International Airport (YUL)

Located in Dorval, about 20 minutes from downtown Montreal, Trudeau is the busiest airport in Quebec. It handles both domestic and international flights, with extensive services including restaurants, shops, and lounges. The airport is well-connected by public transport, including the 747 Express bus service to downtown Montreal.

Contact: +1 514-394-7377.

2. Quebec City Jean Lesage International Airport (YQB)

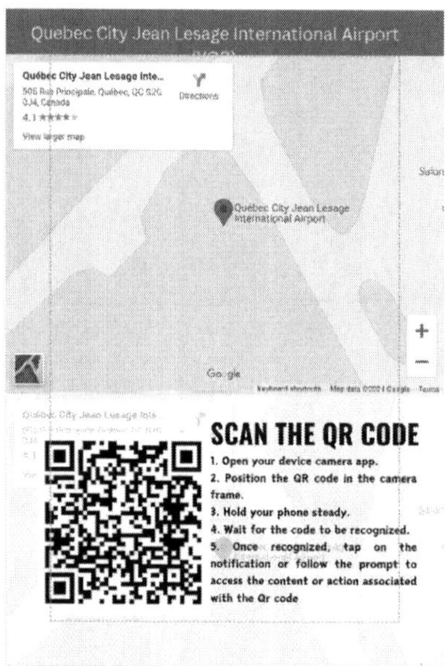

This airport is located 10 miles (16 kilometers) from downtown Quebec City and is the primary gateway to the region. YQB offers direct flights to major Canadian cities, several U.S. destinations, and a few European locations. The airport features modern amenities such as free high-speed internet, various dining options, and a VIP lounge. Public transport includes bus routes 76 and 80, taxis, and rideshare services like Uber.

Contact: +1 418-640-3300.

3. Montreal/Saint-Hubert Airport (YHU)

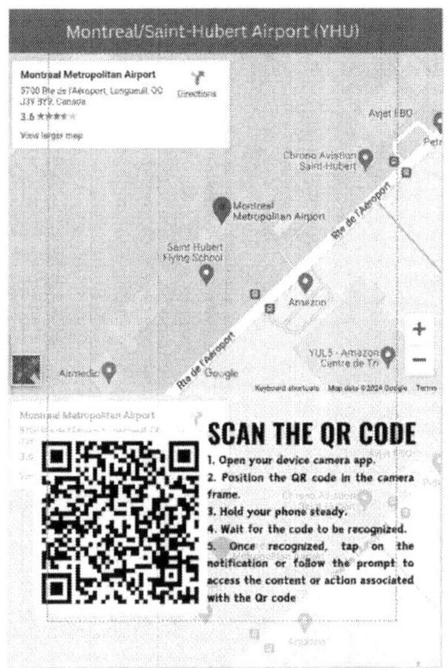

Situated about 15 kilometers from downtown Montreal, this airport primarily handles regional flights and is a convenient alternative for travelers. It is smaller but provides essential services for a comfortable travel experience.

Contact: +1 450-678-6030.

Booking and Costs

When booking your flight to Quebec, consider using comparison websites like Expedia or Kayak to find the best deals. Flights to Quebec City (YQB) often have competitive prices, especially if booked in advance. For example, round-trip flights from major U.S. cities like

New York and Chicago typically range from $300 to $600 depending on the season and availability.

Travel Information

Check-In and Security:

- Most airlines recommend arriving at least 2 hours before domestic flights and 3 hours before international flights.
- Quebec City Jean Lesage International Airport offers a streamlined check-in process and usually short wait times at security checkpoints.

Transportation from Airports:

- **From YUL:** Use the 747 Express bus to reach downtown Montreal or consider renting a car from one of the on-site agencies such as Avis, Budget, or Hertz.
- **From YQB:** Public buses (routes 76 and 80), taxis, and rideshare options are available to get you to downtown Quebec City efficiently.

Enjoying Your Arrival

Once you arrive in Quebec, make sure to take advantage of the amenities offered at these airports. Enjoy a meal at one of the airport restaurants or relax in a lounge if you have some time before exploring the city. Each airport provides a variety of services to ensure you have a comfortable and enjoyable start to your visit.

With these details in hand, your journey to Quebec will be smooth and hassle-free.

B. Train and Bus Options

Traveling to Quebec by train or bus is a convenient and scenic way to experience the region. Whether you prefer the comfort of train travel or the affordability of buses, Quebec offers excellent options for getting around.

Train Travel

Traveling by train in Quebec is a comfortable and efficient option, especially if you're coming from major cities like Montreal or Toronto. The primary operator is VIA Rail Canada, which offers several routes connecting Quebec City with other parts of the country.

VIA Rail Services:

- **Montreal to Quebec City:** This route is very popular and takes approximately 3 hours. VIA Rail operates several trains daily, providing a scenic and relaxing journey through the Quebec countryside. Prices can range from CAD 60 to CAD 216, depending on the class and how early you book. The trains offer amenities such as free Wi-Fi, spacious seating, and onboard meal services.

- **Toronto to Quebec City:** This longer journey takes about 9 hours, but it's a great way to see more of Canada. The train is equipped with comfortable seating, dining options, and Wi-Fi, making it a pleasant travel experience.

Booking and Costs:

- Tickets can be booked online through the VIA Rail website or at train stations. Booking in advance often provides significant savings. VIA Rail also offers various discounts and travel packages that include accommodations and activities.

Stations:

- **Gare du Palais:** The main train station in Quebec City, located at 450 Rue de la Gare-du-Palais. It’s a beautiful historic building that provides easy access to downtown Quebec City.

- **Sainte-Foy Station:** Located at 3255 Chemin de la Gare in the Sainte-Foy–Sillery–Cap-Rouge borough, it serves as an alternative for those in the western part of the city.

Bus Travel

For those looking for a more budget-friendly option, traveling by bus is an excellent choice. Quebec's bus services are extensive, connecting major cities and smaller towns throughout the province.

Orléans Express:

- **Montreal to Quebec City:** Orléans Express operates frequent buses between these two cities, with a travel time of about 3 hours. Tickets typically range from CAD 30 to CAD 60, depending on how early you book and the time of travel. The buses are comfortable and equipped with free Wi-Fi and power outlets.

Intercar:

- **Regional Routes:** Intercar provides services to various regions such as Saguenay, Lac-Saint-Jean, and the North Shore. This is a great option if you're looking to explore beyond the major urban centers.

Greyhound and Other Operators:

- **U.S. to Quebec:** If you're traveling from the United States, Greyhound operates routes to Montreal, where you can easily transfer to a bus or train to Quebec City. This is a cost-effective way to travel long distances while enjoying the scenery.

Booking and Costs:

- Bus tickets can be purchased online through the respective company's website or at bus terminals. Booking early can secure lower prices, and many companies offer student and senior discounts.

Practical Tips

- **Comfort and Convenience:** Both trains and buses in Quebec are designed for comfort, with amenities such as Wi-Fi, power outlets, and ample legroom.

Trains generally offer more space and additional services like dining cars.

- **Accessibility:** VIA Rail and major bus companies provide services for passengers with reduced mobility, ensuring everyone can travel comfortably.
- **Environmental Impact:** Choosing public transportation like trains and buses helps reduce your carbon footprint, making it an eco-friendly option for travel.

C. Driving to Quebec

Driving to Quebec offers a unique opportunity to experience the province's stunning landscapes and charming towns at your own pace. The province is well-connected by major highways, making it accessible from various parts of Canada and the United States.

Major Highways

Highway 20 (Autoroute Jean-Lesage):

- **Route:** Runs along the south shore of the St. Lawrence River, connecting Quebec City to Montreal and continuing towards the eastern part of the province.

- **Scenic Stops:** Along Highway 20, you can stop at picturesque towns like Trois-Rivières, known for its historic sites and waterfront views, and Drummondville, famous for its cultural festivals.

Highway 40 (Autoroute Félix-Leclerc):

- **Route:** Travels along the north shore of the St. Lawrence River, also linking Quebec City and Montreal.
- **Scenic Stops:** This route offers scenic views of the Laurentian Mountains and passes through charming villages like Berthierville and Trois-Rivières. It's a great option if you enjoy scenic drives with plenty of photo opportunities.

Travel Distances and Times

- **From Montreal to Quebec City:** Approximately 153 miles (246 kilometers), about a 2.5-hour drive.
- **From Ottawa to Quebec City:** Approximately 274 miles (441 kilometers), about a 4.5-hour drive.
- **From Toronto to Quebec City:** Approximately 482 miles (776 kilometers), about an 8-hour drive.

- **From Boston to Quebec City:** Approximately 396 miles (637 kilometers), about a 6-hour drive.
- **From New York City to Quebec City:** Approximately 525 miles (845 kilometers), about an 8.5-hour drive.

Tips for Driving

1. Plan Your Route: Use GPS or a reliable map to plan your route in advance. Consider scenic routes for a more enjoyable drive.
2. Check Border Requirements: If driving from the United States, ensure you have the necessary travel documents, such as a valid passport and, if required, a visa or Electronic Travel Authorization (eTA).
3. Weather Conditions: Quebec's weather can be unpredictable, especially in winter. Check the forecast and road conditions before you set out, and be prepared for snow and ice during the colder months.
4. Rest Stops: Plan for rest stops along the way. Quebec's highways have numerous service areas where you can refuel, grab a snack, and take a break.
5. Fuel: Gas stations are plentiful along major highways. However, if you're taking more

remote routes, ensure you fill up your tank before leaving urban areas.

Parking in Quebec

Quebec City:

- **Downtown Parking:** There are several parking garages and lots in downtown Quebec City. Rates vary, but you can expect to pay around CAD 2-4 per hour or CAD 20-30 per day. Some popular spots include the Place d'Youville and Palais Montcalm parking garages.
- **Street Parking:** Metered street parking is available, but be sure to check the signs for time limits and restrictions. Rates are typically around CAD 2-3 per hour.

Montreal:

- **Downtown Parking:** Montreal has numerous parking garages, especially around major attractions and shopping districts. Rates range from CAD 2-5 per hour and CAD 15-25 per day. Popular parking garages include Complexe Desjardins and Place Ville Marie.
- **Street Parking:** Similar to Quebec City, metered parking is available on many

streets. Rates and time limits vary, so check the signs carefully.

Roadside Assistance

- **CAA-Quebec:** If you encounter any issues on the road, CAA-Quebec offers roadside assistance, including towing, battery boosts, and flat tire services. Membership is recommended for peace of mind during your travels.

Contact: +1 800-222-4357.

Chapter 4: Accommodation

A. Hotels and Resorts

1. Fairmont Le Château Frontenac

Welcome to the world's most photographed hotel, the Fairmont Le Château Frontenac! Located in the heart of Old Quebec, this iconic hotel has been a symbol of luxury and history since it opened in 1893. Designed by architect Bruce Price and commissioned by the Canadian Pacific Railway, this grand hotel was built to attract affluent travelers. Its Châteauesque architectural style, inspired by the French Renaissance, features steep roofs, turrets, and ornate detailing, making it a true landmark.

- **Location:** 1 Rue des Carrières, Quebec City, QC G1R 4P5
- **Contact:** +1 418-692-3861
- **How to Reach:** Just a 20-minute drive from Jean Lesage International Airport (YQB). You can easily reach the hotel by taxi or shuttle.
- **Booking:** Rooms can be booked directly through the [Fairmont website](https://www.fairmont.com/frontenac-quebec) or major booking platforms. Rates start around CAD 300 per night.
- **Amenities:** The hotel offers luxurious rooms with breathtaking views of the St. Lawrence River, fine dining at its

multiple restaurants, a spa, an indoor pool, and a fitness center. The hotel also has themed suites honoring historic figures like Winston Churchill and Franklin D. Roosevelt.

- **History:** This hotel has hosted numerous historical events, including the Quebec Conferences of World War II, attended by Winston Churchill and Franklin D. Roosevelt.

2. Hotel Le Germain Montreal

Located in the vibrant downtown area of Montreal, Hotel Le Germain offers a blend of modern luxury and comfort. This boutique hotel is known for its stylish design and exceptional service.

- **Location:** 2050 Rue Mansfield, Montreal, QC H3A 1Y9
- **Contact:** +1 514-849-2050
- **How to Reach:** A short ride from Montreal-Pierre Elliott Trudeau International Airport (YUL), accessible by taxi or the 747 Express bus.
- **Booking:** Reserve a room on the [Hotel Le Germain website](https://www.germainhotels.com/en/le-germain/montreal) or through travel sites like TripAdvisor and Expedia. Rates start at approximately CAD 250 per night.
- **Amenities:** Guests can enjoy a fitness center, complimentary breakfast, and pet-friendly accommodations. The hotel's central location makes it perfect for exploring Montreal's cultural and nightlife scenes.

3. Manoir Hovey

For a serene escape, Manoir Hovey offers a luxurious country retreat on the shores of Lake Massawippi. This Relais & Châteaux property combines historic charm with modern amenities.

- **Location**: 575 Rue Hovey, North Hatley, QC J0B 2C0
- **Contact:** +1 819-842-2421
- **How to Reach:** About a 1.5-hour drive from Montreal, accessible by car or private shuttle.
- **Booking:** Book directly on the [Manoir Hovey website](https://www.manoirhovey.com)

or via luxury travel platforms like Relais & Châteaux. Rates start at CAD 350 per night.

- **Amenities:** The resort features an award-winning restaurant, lakeside activities, a spa, and beautifully landscaped gardens. Ideal for those seeking relaxation and natural beauty.

4. Village Vacances Valcartier

Perfect for families, Village Vacances Valcartier offers fun year-round with North America's largest winter playground, an indoor water park, and the famous Hôtel de Glace (Ice Hotel) during the winter months.

- **Location:** 1860 Boulevard Valcartier, Saint-Gabriel-de-Valcartier, QC G0A 4S0
- **Contact:** +1 888-384-5524
- **How to Reach:** A 30-minute drive from Quebec City, with shuttle services available from the city.
- **Booking:** Reservations can be made on the [Valcartier website](https://www.valcartier.com). Prices start around CAD 150 per night.
- **Amenities:** The resort includes an indoor water park, outdoor winter playground, spa, and various dining options. It's a great place for families looking for adventure and relaxation.

5. Hotel Le Priori

Hotel Le Priori, located in the heart of Old Quebec, offers an intimate and charming stay. This boutique hotel is housed in a historic building and provides personalized service and modern comforts.

- **Location:** 15 Rue Sault-au-Matelot, Quebec City, QC G1K 3Y7
- **Contact:** +1 418-692-3992

- **How to Reach:** A short taxi ride from Jean Lesage International Airport (YQB) or by public transportation.
- **Booking:** Book through the [Hotel Le Priori website](https://www.hotellepriori.com) or via booking sites like TripAdvisor. Rates start at CAD 160 per night.
- **Amenities:** The hotel offers boutique rooms, complimentary breakfast, and free Wi-Fi. It's close to major attractions, making it ideal for exploring Old Quebec.

6. Auberge Saint-Antoine

Auberge Saint-Antoine is a luxurious hotel located in the historic Old Port of Quebec City, offering a blend of contemporary comfort and historical charm.

- **Location:** 8 Rue Saint-Antoine, Quebec City, QC G1K 4C9
- **Contact:** +1 418-692-2211
- **How to Reach:** 20-minute drive from Jean Lesage International Airport (YQB) by taxi.

- **Booking:** [Auberge Saint-Antoine website](https://www.saint-antoine.com). Rates start at CAD 250 per night.
- **Amenities:** Museum artifacts displayed in rooms, fine dining, spa, fitness center.

7. Hotel Nelligan

Located in the heart of Old Montreal, Hotel Nelligan offers a luxurious stay with a historic touch and modern amenities.

- **Location:** 106 Rue Saint-Paul O, Montreal, QC H2Y 1Z3
- **Contact:** +1 514-788-2040
- **How to Reach:** 20-minute drive from Montreal-Pierre Elliott Trudeau International Airport (YUL).
- **Booking:** [Hotel Nelligan website](https://www.hotelnelligan.com). Rates start at CAD 270 per night.
- **Amenities:** Rooftop terrace, fine dining, fitness center, event spaces.

B. Bed and Breakfasts

Staying at a bed and breakfast in Quebec offers a unique and intimate experience, allowing you to enjoy the province's renowned hospitality. Here are some of the best bed and breakfasts you can find in Quebec.

1. Auberge Place d'Armes

Located in the heart of Old Quebec, Auberge Place d'Armes offers a blend of historical charm and modern comforts. Each room is uniquely decorated, reflecting the rich history of the area.

- **Location:** 24 Rue Saint-Anne, Quebec City, QC G1R 3X3
- **Contact:** +1 418-694-9485

- **How to Reach:** A 20-minute drive from Jean Lesage International Airport (YQB).
- **Booking:** Directly through their [website](https://www.aubergeplacedarmes.com). Rates start at CAD 160 per night.
- **Amenities:** Complimentary breakfast, free Wi-Fi, and close proximity to major attractions like Château Frontenac and Dufferin Terrace.

2. Gîte Côté Cour

Gîte Côté Cour is a charming B&B located in a historic building in Old Quebec. Known for its personalized service and warm atmosphere, this B&B offers a cozy retreat with a homemade breakfast served each morning.

- **Location:** 136 Rue Sainte-Angèle, Quebec City, QC G1R 3X8
- **Contact:** +1 418-692-9440
- **How to Reach:** Easily accessible by taxi or public transport from Jean Lesage International Airport (YQB).
- **Booking:** Reserve through their [website](https://www.gitecotecour.com). Rates start at CAD 120 per night.
- **Amenities:** Personalized service, complimentary breakfast, free Wi-Fi, and a welcoming atmosphere.

3. Auberge Saint-Pierre

Auberge Saint-Pierre is located in the Old Port district of Quebec City, combining historic charm with modern amenities. This B&B is perfect for travelers looking for a comfortable and elegant stay.

- **Location:** 79 Rue Saint-Pierre, Quebec City, QC G1K 4A3
- **Contact:** +1 418-694-7981

- **How to Reach:** A short taxi ride from Jean Lesage International Airport (YQB).
- **Booking:** Available on their [website](https://www.auberge-st-pierre.com). Rates start at CAD 180 per night.
- **Amenities:** Complimentary breakfast, free Wi-Fi, cozy lounge, and easy access to nearby attractions like the Museum of Civilization.

4. Le Gite du Hu-Art

For a more secluded and nature-oriented experience, Le Gite du Hu-Art offers a peaceful retreat on the shores of Lake Saint-Charles. This B&B is ideal for those who enjoy outdoor activities and tranquility.

- **Location:** 1673 Avenue du Lac-Saint-Charles, Quebec City, QC G3G 2W5
- **Contact:** +1 418-849-4580
- **How to Reach:** About a 30-minute drive from Jean Lesage International Airport (YQB).
- **Booking:** Book through their [website](https://www.giteduhu-art.com). Rates start at CAD 130 per night.

- **Amenities:** Lakeside location, complimentary breakfast, free use of kayaks and canoes, and beautiful natural surroundings.

5. La Marquise de Bassano

This B&B is located in a Victorian-style house near the Plains of Abraham in Quebec City. La Marquise de Bassano offers a cozy and elegant stay with personalized attention.

- **Location:** 15 Rue des Grisons, Quebec City, QC G1R 4M6
- **Contact:** +1 418-694-1550
- **How to Reach:** A short drive from Jean Lesage International Airport (YQB).
- **Booking:** Reservations can be made on their [website](https://www.lamarquisedebassano.com). Rates start at CAD 140 per night.
- **Amenities:** Victorian charm, complimentary breakfast, free Wi-Fi, and a prime location near historic sites.

C. Vacation Rentals and Hostels

Quebec offers a variety of vacation rentals and hostels that cater to different preferences and budgets. Whether you're looking for the homey feel of an Airbnb or the social environment of a hostel, you'll find plenty of options.

Vacation Rentals

Airbnb Options in Quebec

Staying in an Airbnb provides the comfort of home with the convenience of being close to major attractions. Here are some popular choices:

1. Old Quebec Apartments:

- **Description:** These apartments offer a mix of historic charm and modern amenities. Located in the heart of Old Quebec, they are perfect for those wanting to explore the historic sites on foot.
- **Rates:** Starting from CAD 100 per night.
- **Booking:** Available on [Airbnb](https://www.airbnb.com)

2. Île d'Orléans Cottages:

- **Description:** These charming cottages provide a peaceful retreat with stunning views of the St. Lawrence River. Ideal for families or groups looking to escape the city's hustle and bustle.

- **Rates:** Starting from CAD 150 per night.
- **Booking:** Available on [Airbnb](https://www.airbnb.com).

3. Montreal Downtown Lofts:

- **Description:** These stylish lofts are located in downtown Montreal, close to shops, restaurants, and nightlife. They offer modern amenities and spacious living areas.
- **Rates:** Starting from CAD 120 per night.
- **Booking:** Available on [Airbnb](https://www.airbnb.com).

Hostels

Hostels in Quebec offer budget-friendly accommodations with a social atmosphere. Here are some of the best options:

1. Auberge Internationale de Québec
Located in the heart of Old Quebec, this hostel is perfect for those who want to be close to the action.

- **Location:** 19 Rue Sainte-Ursule, Quebec City, QC G1R 4E1

- **Contact:** +1 418-694-0755
- **Rates:** Dorm beds start at CAD 35 per night.
- **Booking:** Available on the [hostel's website](https://www.hihostels.com).
- **Amenities:** Free Wi-Fi, shared kitchen, common areas, organized social activities.

2. Auberge de la Paix

This modern hostel is centrally located and offers a range of accommodations from dormitory beds to private rooms.

- **Location:** 31 Rue Couillard, Quebec City, QC G1R 3T4
- **Contact:** +1 418-694-0735
- **Rates:** Dorm beds start at CAD 30 per night.
- **Booking:** Available on [Hostelworld](https://www.hostelworld.com) and the [hostel's website](https://www.aubergedelapaix.com).
- **Amenities:** Free Wi-Fi, communal kitchen, backyard patio, lockers, luggage storage.

3. La Belle Planete Backpackers Hostel

A no-frills option located in downtown Quebec City, perfect for budget travelers.

- **Location:** 386 Rue du Pont, Quebec City, QC G1K 6M7
- **Contact:** +1 418-907-9875
- **Rates:** Dorm beds start at CAD 25 per night.
- **Booking:** Available on [Hostelworld](https://www.hostelworld.com) and [Booking.com](https://www.booking.com).
- **Amenities:** Rooftop terrace, communal kitchen, laundry facilities, secure bike storage.

4. Auberge Alternative du Vieux-Montréal

Located in Old Montreal, this hostel offers a vibrant social scene and comfortable accommodations.

- **Location:** 358 Rue Saint-Pierre, Montreal, QC H2Y 2M1
- **Contact:** +1 514-282-8069
- **Rates:** Dorm beds start at CAD 29 per night.
- **Booking:** Available on [Hostelworld](https://www.hostelworld.co

m) and the [hostel's website](https://www.alternativehostel.com).

- **Amenities:** Free Wi-Fi, shared kitchen, common room, bike rentals.

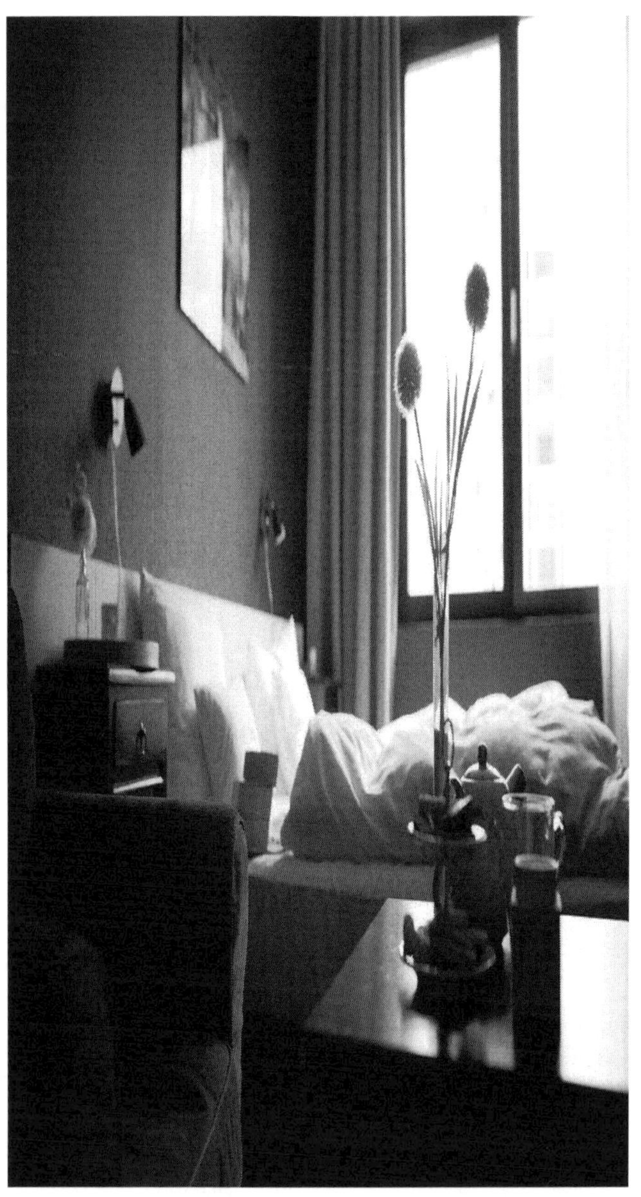

Chapter 5: Top Destinations in Quebec

A. Quebec City

Quebec City, founded in 1608 by Samuel de Champlain, is one of the oldest cities in North America. As the heart of French Canada, it played a significant role in the continent's colonial history. Initially established as a fur trading post, it quickly grew into a fortified city due to its strategic location along the St. Lawrence River. Over the centuries, Quebec City has been a battleground for various European powers, most notably during the Battle of the Plains of Abraham in 1759, which resulted in British control of the city. Today, Quebec City preserves its rich history through its well-preserved architecture and numerous historical sites.

Top Attractions in Quebec City

1. Old Quebec (Vieux-Québec)

- **Description:** A UNESCO World Heritage site, Old Quebec is known for its cobblestone streets, historic buildings, and European charm.
- **Must-See:** Château Frontenac, Place Royale, and the historic Lower Town (Basse-Ville).

2. Château Frontenac

- **Description:** This iconic hotel is a symbol of the city and offers stunning views of the St. Lawrence River.

- **Activities:** Guided tours and dining at one of its fine restaurants.

3. Montmorency Falls

- **Description:** These impressive falls are higher than Niagara Falls and are located just outside the city.
- **Activities:** Cable car rides, hiking trails, and viewing platforms.

4. La Citadelle de Québec

- **Description:** An active military installation and National Historic Site, offering guided tours and museum exhibits.
- **Activities:** Explore the fortifications and enjoy panoramic views of the city.

5. Plains of Abraham

- **Description:** A historic battlefield now transformed into a beautiful urban park.
- **Activities:** Walking tours, museums, and outdoor activities such as picnicking and cross-country skiing.

How to Reach Quebec City

By Air:

- **Jean Lesage International Airport (YQB):** Located about 20 minutes from downtown Quebec City, it offers flights from major North American and European cities.
- **Transportation:** Taxis, shuttles, and rental cars are available at the airport.

By Train:

- **VIA Rail:** Regular services from Montreal, Toronto, and Ottawa. The main station, Gare du Palais, is centrally located in the city.

By Bus:

- **Orléans Express:** Provides comfortable and frequent bus services from various cities in Quebec and neighboring provinces.

What to See and Do

Explore Old Quebec:

- Wander through Quartier Petit-Champlain, visit Place Royale, and take a funicular ride between Upper and Lower Town.

Museums and Galleries:

- **Musée national des beaux-arts du Québec:** Home to a vast collection of Quebec art.
- **Musée de la Civilisation:** Offers interactive exhibits on Quebec's history and culture.

Seasonal Activities:

- **Winter:** Enjoy the Quebec Winter Carnival, tobogganing at Terrasse Dufferin, and ice skating.
- **Summer:** Attend festivals, explore outdoor markets, and take boat tours on the St. Lawrence River.

Where to Eat

Le Continental:

- **Cuisine:** Traditional French with tableside service.
- **Location:** 26 Rue Saint-Louis, Quebec City, QC G1R 3Y9.

Chez Muffy:

- **Cuisine:** Farm-to-table dining in a historic warehouse.
- **Location:** 10 Rue Saint-Antoine, Quebec City, QC G1K 4C9.

Aux Anciens Canadiens:

- **Cuisine:** Traditional Quebecois dishes in a historic building.
- **Location:** 34 Rue Saint-Louis, Quebec City, QC G1R 4P3.

Cost

Accommodation:

- **Budget:** Hostels and budget hotels start at CAD 50 per night.
- **Mid-Range:** Hotels and B&Bs range from CAD 150 to 250 per night.
- **Luxury:** High-end hotels like Château Frontenac start around CAD 300 per night.

Dining:

- **Budget:** CAD 10-20 per meal.
- **Mid-Range:** CAD 25-50 per meal.
- **Luxury:** CAD 75+ per meal at upscale restaurants.

Attractions:

- Many historical sites and parks are free or have minimal entrance fees. Museums and guided tours typically range from CAD 10 to 25.

B. Montreal

Montreal, founded in 1642 as Ville-Marie by French colonists, has grown into one of Canada's most vibrant and culturally diverse cities. Initially established as a missionary colony, it quickly became a hub for the fur trade. Over the centuries, Montreal has evolved into a bustling metropolis known for its rich history, diverse population, and dynamic cultural scene. The city's architecture reflects its historical roots, with influences from French, British, and modern styles. Today, Montreal is a blend of old-world charm and contemporary flair, making it a top destination for travelers from around the world.

Top Attractions in Montreal

1. Old Montreal (Vieux-Montréal)

- **Description:** Explore the cobblestone streets and historic buildings of Old Montreal. Key landmarks include the Notre-Dame Basilica, known for its stunning Gothic Revival architecture, and the Old Port, which offers a variety of recreational activities.
- **Must-See:** Place Jacques-Cartier, Bonsecours Market, and the Pointe-à-Callière Museum.

2. **Mount Royal Park**
   - **Description:** Designed by Frederick Law Olmsted, this expansive park offers hiking trails, lookout points, and winter sports activities. The Mount Royal Chalet provides panoramic views of the city.
   - **Activities:** Hiking, bird watching, picnicking, and skiing in the winter.

3. **Montreal Museum of Fine Arts**
   - **Description:** One of Canada's most prominent art museums, featuring an extensive collection of artworks from various periods and cultures.
   - **Must-See:** The permanent collection and rotating exhibitions showcasing contemporary and classical art.

4. **Underground City (RÉSO)**
   - **Description:** This extensive network of underground walkways connects shopping centers, hotels, and metro stations. It's a great way to navigate the city during harsh weather.
   - **Activities:** Shopping, dining, and exploring art installations during the Art Souterrain festival.

5. Jean-Talon Market

- **Description:** A vibrant public market located in the Little Italy district, offering fresh produce, local specialties, and international foods.
- **Must-See:** Sample local cheeses, charcuterie, and pastries while enjoying the lively market atmosphere.

How to Reach Montreal

By Air:

- **Pierre Elliott Trudeau International Airport (YUL):** The main airport serving Montreal, located about 20 minutes from downtown. It offers numerous domestic and international flights.
- **Transportation:** Taxis, Uber, and the 747 Express bus provide easy access to the city center.

By Train:

- **VIA Rail:** Provides regular services from major Canadian cities such as Toronto and Quebec City. The main station, Gare Centrale, is conveniently located downtown.

By Bus:

- **Greyhound and Megabus:** These services connect Montreal with various North American cities, providing an affordable travel option.

What to See and Do

Explore Old Montreal:

- Wander through Place Jacques-Cartier, visit the Notre-Dame Basilica, and stroll along the Old Port. Don't miss a boat tour on the St. Lawrence River.

Museums and Galleries:

- **Montreal Museum of Fine Arts:** A must-visit for art enthusiasts.
- **Pointe-à-Callière Museum:** Offers fascinating insights into the city's archaeology and history.

Seasonal Activities:

- **Summer:** Enjoy festivals like the Montreal International Jazz Festival and Just for Laughs. Visit outdoor markets and parks.
- **Winter:** Experience the Montreal en Lumière festival, ice skating at Parc La Fontaine, and snowshoeing on Mount Royal.

Where to Eat

Schwartz's Deli:

- **Cuisine:** Famous for its Montreal smoked meat sandwiches.
- **Location:** 3895 Saint-Laurent Blvd, Montreal, QC H2W 1X9.

La Banquise:

- **Cuisine:** Renowned for its poutine, offering a variety of toppings.
- **Location:** 994 Rue Rachel E, Montreal, QC H2J 2J3.

Joe Beef:

- **Cuisine:** A high-end restaurant known for its innovative take on Quebecois cuisine.
- **Location:** 2491 Notre-Dame St W, Montreal, QC H3J 1N6.

Cost

Accommodation:

- **Budget:** Hostels and budget hotels start at CAD 50 per night.
- **Mid-Range:** Hotels range from CAD 150 to 250 per night.

- **Luxury:** High-end hotels like the Ritz-Carlton start around CAD 300 per night.

Dining:

- **Budget:** CAD 10-20 per meal.
- **Mid-Range:** CAD 25-50 per meal.
- **Luxury:** CAD 75+ per meal at upscale restaurants.

Attractions:

- Many parks and outdoor activities are free. Museums and guided tours typically range from CAD 10 to 25.

C. Gatineau

Gatineau, located across the river from Ottawa, is a city rich in history and natural beauty. Originally inhabited by Indigenous peoples, the area became a vital part of the fur trade in the 17th century. As the city developed, it grew into a key administrative and cultural center. Today, Gatineau is known for its picturesque landscapes, cultural institutions, and proximity to Canada's capital.

Top Attractions in Gatineau

1. Canadian Museum of History

- **Description:** This is Canada's most visited museum, offering a comprehensive look at the country's history and heritage. It features exhibits on Indigenous cultures, Canadian history, and special exhibitions.

- **Must-See:** The Grand Hall, which houses the world's largest indoor collection of totem poles.
- **Location:** 100 Laurier Street, Gatineau, QC K1A 0M8
- **Contact:** +1 819-776-7000.

2. Gatineau Park

- **Description:** A stunning natural reserve offering a variety of outdoor activities such as hiking, biking, and skiing. The park is home to beautiful lakes, scenic lookouts, and rich wildlife.
- **Activities:** Hiking trails, picnic areas, and winter sports.
- **Location:** Accessible via multiple entrances, with the main visitor center at 33 Scott Road, Chelsea, QC J9B 1R5.

3. Jacques Cartier Park

- **Description:** Located along the Ottawa River, this park is famous for hosting Winterlude, an annual winter festival featuring ice sculptures, skating, and snow slides.
- **Activities:** Boating, picnicking, and seasonal festivals.
- **Location:** 164 Laurier Street, Gatineau, QC J8X 3W1.

4. Casino du Lac-Leamy

- **Description:** This popular casino offers gaming, fine dining, and live entertainment. It's a great place for a night out with friends or to try your luck at the tables.
- **Activities:** Casino games, shows, and gourmet restaurants.
- **Location:** 1 Boulevard du Casino, Gatineau, QC J8Y 6W3.

5. Parc du Lac Leamy

- **Description:** A serene park with a lake ideal for swimming, kayaking, and relaxing on the beach. It's a peaceful getaway in the heart of the city.
- **Activities:** Beach, playgrounds, and picnic spots.
- **Location:** 100 Atawe Street, Gatineau, QC J8Y 6V5.

How to Reach Gatineau

By Air:

- **Ottawa Macdonald-Cartier International Airport (YOW):** Located about 20 minutes from Gatineau, this is the nearest major airport. It offers numerous domestic and international flights.

- **Transportation:** Taxis, Uber, and rental cars are readily available at the airport.

By Train:

- **Via Rail:** Provides service to Ottawa, where you can then take a short taxi or bus ride to Gatineau.

By Bus:

- **Greyhound and Local Buses:** Connect Gatineau with Ottawa and other major cities in Quebec and Ontario.

What to See and Do

Explore Cultural Sites:

- Visit the Canadian Museum of History for an in-depth look at Canada's past.
- Enjoy the exhibitions and collections at the National Gallery of Canada, located just across the river in Ottawa.

Outdoor Activities:

- Spend a day hiking or skiing in Gatineau Park.
- Relax at the beaches and parks along the Ottawa River.

Seasonal Activities:

- **Winter:** Experience Winterlude in Jacques Cartier Park with its ice sculptures and snow activities.
- **Summer:** Enjoy outdoor concerts, boating, and picnics in the city's numerous parks.

Where to Eat

Les Brasseurs du Temps:

- **Cuisine:** Craft brewery with a menu of pub favorites.
- **Location:** 170 Montcalm Street, Gatineau, QC J8X 2M2.

Bistro CoqLicorne:

- **Cuisine:** French-inspired dishes using local ingredients.
- **Location:** 59 Rue Laval, Gatineau, QC J8X 3H1.

Le Cellier:

- **Cuisine:** Upscale dining with an extensive wine list.

Location: 1039 Boulevard Saint-Joseph, Gatineau, QC J8Z 1T3.

Cost

Accommodation:

- **Budget:** Hostels and budget hotels start at CAD 60 per night.
- **Mid-Range:** Hotels range from CAD 120 to 200 per night.
- **Luxury:** High-end hotels and resorts start at CAD 250 per night.

Dining:

- **Budget:** CAD 10-20 per meal.
- **Mid-Range:** CAD 25-50 per meal.
- **Luxury:** CAD 75+ per meal at upscale restaurants.

Attractions:

- Many parks and outdoor activities are free. Museums and guided tours typically range from CAD 10 to 25.

D. Charlevoix

Charlevoix, located along the north shore of the St. Lawrence River, is a region rich in history and natural beauty. Its name originates from Pierre-François-Xavier de Charlevoix, a French Jesuit explorer and historian who visited the area in the early 18th century. The region has been a popular destination for tourists for over 200 years, known for its picturesque landscapes, quaint villages, and vibrant arts scene. Today, Charlevoix continues to attract visitors with its blend of cultural experiences and outdoor adventures.

Top Attractions in Charlevoix

1. Parc National des Hautes-Gorges-de-la-Rivière-Malbaie

- **Description:** This national park is renowned for its stunning landscapes, featuring deep valleys, towering cliffs, and the Malbaie River. It's a paradise for hikers, kayakers, and nature lovers.
- **Activities:** Hiking, kayaking, wildlife observation.
- **Location:** Accessible from Route 138, near the town of Clermont.

2. Le Massif de Charlevoix

- **Description:** Known for having the highest vertical drop east of the Rockies, this ski resort offers breathtaking views and a range of winter sports.
- **Activities:** Skiing, snowboarding, sledding, mountain biking.
- **Location:** 1350 Rue Principale, Petite-Rivière-Saint-François, QC G0A 2L0.

3. Baie-Saint-Paul

- **Description:** A charming village known for its art galleries, boutiques, and restaurants. It's a hub for artists and offers a picturesque setting for visitors.

- **Must-See:** Musée d'art contemporain de Baie-Saint-Paul, Rue Saint-Jean-Baptiste.
- **Activities:** Art gallery tours, shopping, dining.

4. Casino de Charlevoix

- **Description:** Located in La Malbaie, this casino offers gaming, dining, and entertainment. It's housed in the luxurious Fairmont Le Manoir Richelieu.
- **Activities:** Casino games, live shows, fine dining.
- **Location:** 183 Rue Richelieu, La Malbaie, QC G5A 1X8.

5. Whale Watching

- **Description:** The St. Lawrence River is a prime spot for whale watching. Tours are available to see minke whales, belugas, and even blue whales.
- **Season:** Best from spring to fall.
- **Providers:** Croisières AML offers popular whale-watching tours.

How to Reach Charlevoix

By Air:

- **Jean Lesage International Airport (YQB):** The closest major airport, located about 1.5 hours from Charlevoix by car.
- **Transportation:** Rental cars and shuttle services are available at the airport.

By Train:

- **Train de Charlevoix:** Offers a scenic train ride between Quebec City and La Malbaie, passing through picturesque landscapes.

By Car:

- **Route 138:** The main highway connecting Quebec City to Charlevoix, offering stunning views along the St. Lawrence River.

What to See and Do

Explore the Parks:

- Hike through Parc National des Grands-Jardins and Parc National des Hautes-Gorges-de-la-Rivière-Malbaie.
- Enjoy outdoor activities like canoeing, bird watching, and star gazing.

Cultural Experiences:

- Visit art galleries in Baie-Saint-Paul and attend performances at Domaine Forget.
- Explore local history at the Charlevoix Maritime Museum and Espace muséal petites franciscaines de Marie.

Seasonal Activities:

- **Winter:** Skiing, snowshoeing, and sledding at Le Massif de Charlevoix.
- **Summer:** Whale watching, hiking, and golfing at Fairmont Le Manoir Richelieu Golf Club.

Where to Eat

Le Mouton Noir:

- **Cuisine:** French-inspired farm-to-table dining.
- **Location:** 43 Rue Sainte-Anne, Baie-Saint-Paul, QC G3Z 1P8.

Restaurant Le Saint-Pub:

- **Cuisine:** Local brews and pub fare.
- **Location:** 2 Rue Racine, Baie-Saint-Paul, QC G3Z 2P8.

Auberge des Falaises:

- **Cuisine:** Fine dining with a focus on local ingredients.
- **Location:** 250 Chemin des Falaises, La Malbaie, QC G5A 2V2【198†source】.

Cost

Accommodation:

- **Budget:** B&Bs and budget inns start at CAD 80 per night.
- **Mid-Range:** Hotels and lodges range from CAD 150 to 250 per night.
- **Luxury:** High-end resorts and boutique hotels start around CAD 300 per night.

Dining:

- **Budget:** CAD 10-20 per meal.
- **Mid-Range:** CAD 25-50 per meal.
- **Luxury:** CAD 75+ per meal at upscale restaurants.

Attractions:

- Many outdoor activities and park entrances are free or have minimal fees. Tours and guided experiences typically range from CAD 20 to 50.

E. Eastern Townships

The Eastern Townships, or "Les Cantons-de-l'Est," were originally settled by American Loyalists fleeing the Revolutionary War. Over the years, the area has evolved into a picturesque region known for its rolling hills, charming villages, and vibrant cultural scene. Nestled between the Appalachian Mountains and the US border, the Eastern Townships are a haven for outdoor enthusiasts and those seeking a peaceful retreat.

Top Attractions in the Eastern Townships

1. Parc National du Mont-Mégantic

- **Description:** Renowned for its clear night skies, this park is home to the ASTROLab and the first International Dark Sky Reserve. It offers excellent stargazing opportunities, along with hiking and wildlife viewing.
- **Activities:** Stargazing, hiking, camping.
- **Location:** Accessible via Route 212 near Notre-Dame-des-Bois.

2. Brome Lake (Lac-Brome)

- **Description:** This area combines several villages around Brome Lake, known for its art galleries, antique shops, and beautiful lakeside views. It's a popular spot for water sports and relaxation.
- **Activities:** Boating, swimming, shopping, and dining.
- **Location:** Central location within the Townships, easily accessible by car.

3. Wine Route (Route des Vins)

- **Description:** This scenic route connects about 20 vineyards, offering wine tasting and tours. It's a great way to explore the local wine culture and enjoy the beautiful countryside.
- **Activities:** Wine tasting, vineyard tours, dining.
- **Location:** Spanning from Dunham to Magog, accessible by car.

4. Parc de la Gorge de Coaticook

- **Description:** Famous for its impressive suspension bridge, this park offers hiking, camping, and a multimedia night walk called "Foresta Lumina."
- **Activities:** Hiking, camping, exploring "Foresta Lumina."

- **Location:** 400 St-Marc Street, Coaticook, QC J1A 2T7.

5. Abbey of Saint-Benoît-du-Lac

- **Description:** A serene monastery located on the shores of Lake Memphremagog. The Abbey is known for its Gregorian chants and homemade products like cheese and cider.
- **Activities:** Tours, attending mass, shopping for local products.
- **Location:** 1 Rue Principale, Saint-Benoît-du-Lac, QC J0B 2M0.

How to Reach the Eastern Townships

By Air:

- **Jean Lesage International Airport (YQB):** Located in Quebec City, about 1.5-2 hours by car to the Eastern Townships.
- **Montreal-Pierre Elliott Trudeau International Airport (YUL):** About 1-2 hours by car from most destinations within the Eastern Townships.

By Car:

- **Route 112 and Autoroute 10:** Main highways connecting Montreal to the

Eastern Townships, offering scenic drives through the countryside.

What to See and Do

Explore Scenic Routes:

- Drive or bike along the Chemin des Cantons to experience beautiful views of the fall foliage, historic homes, and quaint villages.

Outdoor Activities:

- Visit Mont-Orford National Park for hiking, biking, and skiing.
- Enjoy water sports on Lake Memphremagog or Brome Lake.

Cultural Experiences:

- Attend a concert at Orford Musique, a renowned music academy and performance venue.
- Visit local markets like the Stratford Farmers' Market to experience regional produce and crafts.

Where to Eat

Auberge West Brome:

- **Cuisine:** Farm-to-table dining with a focus on local ingredients.
- **Location:** 128 Route 139, West Brome, QC J0E 2P0.

Le Hatley at Manoir Hovey:

- **Cuisine:** Upscale dining with a focus on regional flavors.
- **Location:** 575 Rue Hovey, North Hatley, QC J0B 2C0.

Bistro 4 Saisons:

- **Cuisine:** French-inspired cuisine with seasonal ingredients.
- **Location:** 4940 Chemin du Parc, Orford, QC J1X 7N9.

Cost

Accommodation:

- **Budget:** Hostels and motels start at CAD 70 per night.
- **Mid-Range:** Hotels and inns range from CAD 120 to 200 per night.
- **Luxury:** Resorts and boutique hotels start at CAD 250 per night.

Dining:

- **Budget:** CAD 10-20 per meal.

- **Mid-Range:** CAD 25-50 per meal.
- **Luxury:** CAD 75+ per meal at upscale restaurants.

Attractions:

- Many outdoor activities and park entrances are free or have minimal fees. Tours and guided experiences typically range from CAD 20 to 50.

Chapter 6: Itinerary Planning

A. Sample 3-Day Itinerary

Day 1: Exploring Old Quebec

Morning:

Château Frontenac: Start your day with a visit to the iconic Château Frontenac, one of the most photographed hotels in the world. Enjoy a guided tour to learn about its history and architecture.

- **Location:** 1 Rue des Carrières, Quebec City, QC G1R 4P5
- **Hours:** Tours available daily
- **Cost:** Approximately CAD 22 per person
- **Contact:** +1 418-692-3861

Lunch:

Le Chic Shack: Just a short walk from Château Frontenac, this restaurant offers gourmet poutine, burgers, and milkshakes.

- **Location:** 15 Rue du Fort, Quebec City, QC G1R 3W9
- **Hours:** 11 AM - 9 PM daily
- **Cost:** CAD 15-25 per person

Afternoon:

Old Quebec (Vieux-Québec): Wander through the cobblestone streets of Old Quebec. Visit Place Royale, the birthplace of French civilization in North America, and explore the Petit Champlain District with its charming boutiques and cafes.

- **Top Sights:** Notre-Dame de Québec Basilica-Cathedral, Quartier Petit Champlain, and La Fresque des Québécois mural

Dinner:

Aux Anciens Canadiens: Enjoy a traditional Quebecois meal in a historic setting.

- **Location:** 34 Rue Saint-Louis, Quebec City, QC G1R 4P3
- **Hours:** 11:30 AM - 9 PM daily
- **Cost:** CAD 30-50 per person

Day 2: Culture and Nature

Morning:

Musée de la Civilisation: Dive into Quebec's history and culture at this engaging museum.

- **Location:** 85 Rue Dalhousie, Quebec City, QC G1K 8R2
- **Hours:** 10 AM - 5 PM daily
- **Cost:** CAD 16 per adult
- **Contact:** +1 418-643-2158

Lunch:

Chez Muffy: Located in the Auberge Saint-Antoine, this farm-to-table restaurant offers a cozy atmosphere and delicious cuisine.

- **Location:** 10 Rue Saint-Antoine, Quebec City, QC G1K 4C9
- **Hours:** 11:30 AM - 2 PM for lunch, 6 PM - 10 PM for dinner
- **Cost:** CAD 40-60 per person

Afternoon:

Montmorency Falls: Just a short drive from Quebec City, these falls are higher than Niagara Falls and offer spectacular views.

- **Activities:** Take the cable car to the top, walk across the suspension bridge, or hike the surrounding trails.

- **Location:** 5300 Boulevard Sainte-Anne, Quebec City, QC G1C 1S1
- **Hours:** 9 AM - 5 PM daily
- **Cost:** CAD 14 per adult for the cable car
- **Contact:** +1 418-663-3330

Dinner:

Le Saint-Amour: Treat yourself to an exquisite French dining experience.
Location**: 48 Rue Sainte-Ursule, Quebec City, QC G1R 4E2

- **Hours:** 6 PM - 9 PM daily
- **Cost:** CAD 60-100 per person

Day 3: Day Trip and Relaxation

Morning:

Île d'Orléans: Take a short drive or ferry ride to this beautiful island known for its local produce and charming villages.

- **Activities:** Visit local farms and vineyards, taste fresh berries, and explore historic churches.
- **Top Stops:** Vignoble Sainte-Pétronille, Cassis Monna & Filles, and the Chocolaterie de l'île d'Orléans

Lunch:

La Goéliche: Enjoy a meal with a view of the St. Lawrence River.

- **Location:** 22 Chemin du Quai, Sainte-Pétronille, QC G0A 4C0
- **Hours:** 11:30 AM - 2 PM for lunch, 5 PM - 9 PM for dinner
- **Cost:** CAD 30-50 per person

Afternoon:

Relax in Quebec City: Return to the city and unwind. Visit a café like **Café La Maison Smith** for a coffee and pastry.

- **Location:** 23 Rue Notre-Dame, Quebec City, QC G1K 4E9
- Hours**:** 7 AM - 7 PM daily
- **Cost:** CAD 10-20 per person

Evening:

Ghost Tours of Quebec: End your trip with a spooky and entertaining ghost tour through Old Quebec.

- **Location:** Meeting point varies, check [Ghost Tours of Quebec](https://www.ghosttoursofquebec.com) for details
- **Hours:** Tours at 8 PM from May to October
- **Cost:** CAD 22 per adult
- **Contact:** +1 418-692-9770

B. Sample 7-Day Itinerary

Day 1: Arrival and Montreal Exploration

Morning:

- **Arrival in Montreal:** Fly into Montreal-Pierre Elliott Trudeau International Airport (YUL). Depending on your arrival time, check into your hotel.
- **Hotel Recommendation:** Best Western Plus Montreal Downtown for mid-range stays or Boxotel for a luxury experience.

Afternoon:

- **Old Montreal (Vieux-Montréal):** Explore the cobblestone streets, visit the Notre-Dame Basilica, and stroll along the Old Port.
- **Lunch:** Try a smoked meat sandwich at Schwartz's Deli.

Evening:

- **Dinner:** Enjoy French cuisine at Le Club Chasse et Pêche.
- **Night:** Relax at your hotel or explore Montreal's vibrant nightlife.

Day 2: Montreal Highlights

Morning:

- **Mount Royal Park:** Hike or take a leisurely walk up to the Kondiaronk Belvedere for panoramic views of the city.

Afternoon:

- **Montreal Museum of Fine Arts:** Visit this extensive collection of art from various periods and cultures.
- **Lunch:** Dine at La Banquise, famous for its poutine.

Evening:

- **Dinner:** Enjoy a meal at Au Pied de Cochon, known for hearty Quebecois dishes.
- **Activity:** Explore the Underground City (RÉSO) for some evening shopping or a casual stroll.

Day 3: Drive to Quebec City

Morning:

- **Travel:** Drive or take a bus from Montreal to Quebec City (approximately 3 hours).

Afternoon:

- **Old Quebec:** Check into your hotel and start exploring the historic landmarks. Visit Château Frontenac, Dufferin Terrace, and Place Royale.
- **Lunch:** Eat at one of the city's famous bakeries like Paillard.

Evening:

- **Dinner:** Dine at Aux Anciens Canadiens for traditional Quebecois cuisine.
- **Night:** Stroll through the Quartier Petit Champlain for a nightcap or dessert.

Day 4: Quebec City Exploration

Morning:

- **Citadel of Quebec:** Visit this active military installation and National Historic Site.

Afternoon:

- **Plains of Abraham:** Explore this historic battlefield turned urban park.
- **Lunch:** Have a meal at Le Saint-Amour.

Evening:

- **Dinner:** Try a gourmet experience at Restaurant Légende.

- **Activity:** Take a sunset ferry ride to Lévis for stunning views of Quebec City from the river.

Day 5: Day Trip to Île d'Orléans

Morning:

- **Travel:** Drive or take a ferry to Île d'Orléans.
- **Activity:** Visit local farms, vineyards, and taste fresh produce.

Afternoon:

- **Lunch:** Enjoy local dishes at La Goéliche in Sainte-Pétronille.
- **Activities:** Explore the Mauvide-Genest Manor and the Saint-François-de-Sales church.

Evening:

- **Return:** Head back to Quebec City and have dinner at a local restaurant like Le Lapin Sauté.

Day 6: Charlevoix Region

Morning:

- **Travel:** Drive to the Charlevoix region.

- **Activities:** Visit Parc national des Grands-Jardins and explore the scenic trails and lookouts.

Afternoon:

- **Lunch:** Eat at Le Mouton Noir in Baie-Saint-Paul.
- **Activities:** Visit the Musée d'art contemporain de Baie-Saint-Paul and stroll through the village.

Evening:

- **Return:** Drive back to Quebec City for dinner and relaxation.

Day 7: Departure

Morning:

- **Last-minute Shopping and Sightseeing:** Visit any remaining sites or do some last-minute shopping in Quebec City.
- **Breakfast:** Enjoy a final Quebecois breakfast at Le Hobbit or La Maison Smith.

Afternoon:

- **Travel:** Head to the airport for your departure.

C. Customizing Your Itinerary

Customizing your itinerary allows you to create a travel plan that perfectly suits your preferences and interests. Here are some tips and ideas to help you personalize your Quebec adventure.

Focus Areas for Customization

1. Historical and Cultural Enthusiasts

If you have a passion for history and culture, focus on Quebec City's rich heritage and Montreal's vibrant arts scene.

- **Quebec City:** Spend extra time exploring Old Quebec, the Citadel, and the Plains of Abraham. Visit the Musée de l'Amérique Francophone for insights into the French-speaking world.
- **Montreal:** Dive deep into the cultural hubs of Old Montreal, the Montreal Museum of Fine Arts, and the Biodome. Don't miss the historic architecture of the Notre-Dame Basilica and the Pointe-à-Callière Museum.

2. Outdoor Adventurers

For those who love the great outdoors, Quebec offers plenty of opportunities for adventure.

- **Quebec City:** Take advantage of the hiking trails at Montmorency Falls and the outdoor activities available in Jacques-Cartier National Park.
- **Eastern Townships:** Go hiking, biking, and kayaking in the beautiful landscapes of Mont-Orford National Park and Parc de la Gorge de Coaticook.

3. Food and Wine Lovers

Quebec's culinary scene is a treat for food enthusiasts.

- **Wine Route:** Spend a day or two exploring the Route des Vins in the Eastern Townships, sampling wines from local vineyards like Vignoble de l'Orpailleur and Domaine Pinnacle.
- **Farm-to-Table Experiences:** Enjoy dining at farm-to-table restaurants such as Le Hatley at Manoir Hovey and Bistro 4 Saisons in the Eastern Townships.

Family-Friendly Itinerary

Day 1-2: Quebec City

- **Old Quebec:** Explore the historic district, visit the Citadel, and enjoy a family-friendly tour of Château Frontenac.
- **Montmorency Falls:** Take the kids on the cable car and enjoy a picnic by the falls.

Day 3-4: Montreal

- **Biodome and Insectarium:** Spend a day exploring these interactive museums that are perfect for children.
- **Mount Royal Park:** Enjoy a family hike and a picnic with stunning views of the city.

Day 5-6: Eastern Townships

- **Parc de la Gorge de Coaticook:** Walk across the suspension bridge and experience the "Foresta Lumina" night walk.
- **Brome Lake:** Rent kayaks or paddleboards and enjoy water activities with the family.

Day 7: Return to Quebec City or Montreal for departure.

Romantic Getaway Itinerary

Day 1-2: Quebec City

- **Old Quebec:** Stroll through the charming streets, visit Place Royale, and dine at cozy restaurants like Le Saint-Amour.
- **Île d'Orléans:** Take a romantic day trip to the island, enjoy wine tasting, and have a picnic with river views.

Day 3-4: Charlevoix

- **Le Massif de Charlevoix:** Experience scenic views and outdoor activities like hiking or skiing, depending on the season.
- **Baie-Saint-Paul:** Stay at a quaint inn, explore art galleries, and enjoy a romantic dinner at Le Mouton Noir.

Day 5-6: Montreal

- **Old Montreal:** Walk hand-in-hand through the historic district, visit the Notre-Dame Basilica, and dine at a French bistro.
- **Mount Royal:** Take a sunset hike and enjoy the panoramic view from the top.

Day 7: Relax at Spa Bota Bota, a floating spa on the St. Lawrence River, before departure.

Day Trips and Excursions

From Quebec City:

- **Montmorency Falls:** A short drive or bus ride from Quebec City, perfect for a half-day trip.
- **Île d'Orléans:** Enjoy a scenic drive, local food tastings, and charming villages.

From Montreal:

- **Eastern Townships:** About an hour and a half drive from Montreal, ideal for exploring vineyards and quaint towns.
- **Ottawa/Gatineau:** A two-hour drive for a day trip to Canada's capital and its museums.

Planning Tips

- **Flexibility:** Keep some flexibility in your schedule to accommodate spontaneous discoveries or local events.
- **Local Events:** Check local event calendars for festivals, markets, and

special exhibitions that may enhance your trip.

- **Transportation:** Consider renting a car if you plan to explore areas outside the main cities, especially for regions like Charlevoix and the Eastern Townships.

D. Day Trips and Excursions

From Quebec City

1. Montmorency Falls

- **Travel Time:** 15 minutes by car
- **Description:** Higher than Niagara Falls, Montmorency Falls offers stunning views and a range of activities including cable car rides, hiking trails, and a suspension bridge.
- **Activities:** Hiking, picnicking, and photography. In winter, the falls create a beautiful frozen landscape.

2. Île d'Orléans

- **Travel Time:** 30 minutes by car
- **Description:** Known as the "Garden of Quebec," this island is famous for its local produce, vineyards, and charming villages.

- **Activities:** Wine tasting, visiting local farms, and exploring historic churches. Perfect for a leisurely day trip.

3. Baie-Saint-Paul

- **Travel Time:** 1 hour by car
- **Description:** A picturesque town in the Charlevoix region, Baie-Saint-Paul is known for its art galleries, local boutiques, and gourmet dining.
- **Activities:** Explore Saint-Jean-Baptiste Street, visit the Musée d'Art Contemporain, and enjoy local cuisine at Le Saint-Pub microbrewery.

4. Parc National des Hautes-Gorges-de-la-Rivière-Malbaie

- **Travel Time:** 2 hours by car
- **Description:** This national park offers breathtaking landscapes with deep valleys and towering cliffs. Ideal for outdoor enthusiasts.
- **Activities:** Hiking, biking, and in winter, snowshoeing and ice climbing. A great spot for nature lovers.

5. Grosse Île and the Irish Memorial National Historic Site

- **Travel Time:** 45 minutes to the Berthier-sur-Mer ferry, followed by a short ferry ride
- **Description:** A historic site that served as a quarantine station for Irish immigrants in the 19th century.
- **Activities:** Guided tours, hiking, and exploring historical exhibits. The site is open from May to October.

6. Wendake

- **Travel Time:** 25 minutes by car
- **Description:** An Indigenous village that offers a rich cultural experience with the Huron-Wendat Nation.
- **Activities:** Visit the Musée Huron-Wendat, join craft workshops, and experience traditional Huron-Wendat performances.

From Montreal

1. Mont Tremblant

- **Travel Time:** 1.5 hours by car
- **Description:** A popular destination for skiing in winter and hiking in summer. Mont Tremblant offers beautiful natural scenery and outdoor activities.

- **Activities:** Skiing, hiking, and mountain biking. Enjoy the scenic views and the lively village atmosphere.

2. Omega Park
    - **Travel Time:** 1.5 hours by car
    - **Description:** A wildlife park that offers a safari-like experience with Canadian animals such as bison, bears, and wolves.
    - **Activities:** Self-drive tours, hiking trails, and photo opportunities. A great destination for families and nature enthusiasts.

3. Iles-de-Boucherville National Park
    - **Travel Time:** 30 minutes by car
    - **Description:** A chain of islands offering a peaceful escape with activities like kayaking, hiking, and wildlife viewing.
    - **Activities:** Canoeing, hiking, and snowshoeing in winter. Ideal for a day immersed in nature close to the city.

4. Laurentians
    - **Travel Time:** 1 hour by car
    - **Description:** Known for its beautiful landscapes, the Laurentians are perfect

for a self-guided driving tour with plenty of hiking opportunities.

- **Activities:** Hiking, skiing, and exploring small towns. The region is known for its tranquility and natural beauty.

5. Ottawa

- **Travel Time:** 2 hours by car
- **Description:** Canada's capital city, rich in history and culture with numerous museums and historic sites.
- **Activities:** Visit Parliament Hill, the National Gallery of Canada, and the Canadian Museum of History. Enjoy a day exploring the capital's landmarks and attractions.

LE FEU
SACRÉ

Chapter 7: Transportation within Quebec

A. Public Transportation

Quebec City

Quebec City boasts a well-organized public transportation system operated by the Réseau de Transport de la Capitale (RTC). The city's bus network is extensive, with regular routes covering major areas and express services ensuring quick commutes during rush hours. The RTC's Métrobuses, numbered in the 800s, run frequently and are a convenient option for tourists exploring the city without a strict schedule.

Fares and Payment Methods:

- **Cash:** Pay directly on the bus, but exact change is required.
- **Occasional Card:** Offers discounted fares compared to cash payments. Cards can be purchased at various retailers across the city.
- **Mobile App:** The RTC Nomade app allows for purchasing fares and provides real-time updates on bus schedules and routes. This app is available on both Google Play and the App Store.

Accessibility:

Many RTC buses are equipped to accommodate passengers with limited mobility. Features include low-floor buses that can lower to curb height and priority seating areas.

Special Services:

- **Airport Shuttle:** Bus route 80 connects Jean Lesage International Airport with the city center, making it easy for travelers to access downtown Quebec City.
- **Event Shuttles:** During major events, RTC provides shuttle services to

facilitate transportation from various parts of the city to event venues.

Montreal

Montreal's public transportation system, operated by the Société de transport de Montréal (STM), includes a comprehensive network of buses and metro lines. The metro system is particularly efficient, with four lines covering extensive parts of the city. The STM also introduced the Réseau express métropolitain (REM), a new automated light rail network enhancing connectivity across Greater Montreal.

Fares and Payment Methods:

- **Single-Ride Tickets:** CAD 3.50 for both bus and metro, available at stations.
- **Opus Card**:** A reloadable transit card for frequent travelers, offering day passes and monthly subscriptions.

Safety and Accessibility:

Montreal's public transportation is considered very safe, even at night. The "Between Stops" service allows women traveling at night to request stops closer to their destination for added safety. Most buses and metro stations are equipped to accommodate passengers with disabilities.

Additional Services:

- **Airport Shuttle:** The 747 Express bus provides a direct connection between Montreal-Pierre Elliott Trudeau International Airport and downtown Montreal, operating 24/7.

B. Renting a Car

Renting a car in Quebec offers the flexibility to explore the region at your own pace, whether you're navigating the streets of Quebec City, Montreal, or venturing into the scenic countryside.

Major Car Rental Companies

Quebec is served by several major car rental companies, providing a range of vehicles to suit different needs and budgets. Here are some popular options:

Enterprise Rent-A-Car:

- **Locations:** Quebec City Jean Lesage International Airport (YQB), various neighborhood locations including

Ancienne-Lorette, Beauport, and Delta Hotel.

- **Rates:** Starting around CAD 85 per day, with cheaper rates available in off-peak months such as May.
- **Booking:** You can book online through the [Enterprise website](https://www.enterprise.ca).

Special Services: Offers curbside rentals and delivery at select locations.

Avis:

- **Locations:** Quebec City Jean Lesage International Airport, downtown Quebec City.
- **Rates:** Competitive rates starting from CAD 85 per day, with special deals available through their [website](https://www.avis.ca).
- **Booking:** Reservations can be made online, and they offer free pickup service within the city.

Budget:

- **Locations:** Quebec City Airport and several neighborhood locations.
- **Rates:** Prices start around CAD 87 per day, with seasonal discounts.

- **Booking:** Book through the [Budget website](https://www.budget.com).
- **Special Services:** Budget offers cross-border rentals and various vehicle types including SUVs and luxury cars.

Tips for Renting a Car

1. Book in Advance: To get the best rates, especially during peak travel seasons like summer, it's advisable to book your rental car well in advance. Prices tend to be lower if you book at least a month ahead.

2. Compare Prices: Use comparison websites like Kayak or Discover Cars to find the best deals and read reviews of different rental companies to ensure good service and reliability.

3. Check for Discounts: Many rental companies offer discounts for members of certain organizations (like AAA or CAA), or through travel clubs and frequent flyer programs.

4. Insurance: Verify what insurance coverage is included with your rental. Your personal auto insurance or credit card may offer rental coverage, which can save you money on additional insurance costs.

5. Fuel Policy: Be aware of the fuel policy when you rent the car. Some companies require you to return the car with a full tank, while others might offer a pre-purchase fuel option.

Cost and Availability

Car rental prices in Quebec City and Montreal can vary significantly depending on the season and demand. On average, you can expect to pay between CAD 46 to CAD 104 per day. The cheapest months to rent are typically April and May, while prices peak in August.

Off-Peak Rates:

- **May:** Approximately CAD 46 per day.

Peak Rates:

- **August:** Approximately CAD 104 per day.

C. Cycling and Walking

Cycling

Cycling is an excellent way to explore Quebec, offering both urban and scenic routes for riders of all levels. Here's a guide to some of the best cycling paths and resources in Quebec City and beyond.

Quebec City:

1. Corridor du Littoral: This 50 km flat trail runs along the St. Lawrence River, connecting Old Quebec to Montmorency Falls. It's part of the Route Verte, North America's longest network of bike paths. The route offers stunning views and is perfect for leisurely rides.

2. Île d'Orléans: A popular destination for cyclists, this island provides a scenic 66.5 km route around its perimeter. The ride features beautiful countryside, farmers' stalls, and wineries. The roads are shared with motor vehicles, but traffic is generally light and respectful towards cyclists.

Bike Rentals:

- **Echo Sports:** Offers four-hour and full-day rentals, including electric bikes.
- **Cyclo Services:** Provides similar rental options and is conveniently located near Old Port and the St. Lawrence River.

Bike Tours:

- **Old Quebec Cycling Tour:** A guided tour through historic areas including Place Royale and Quartier Petit Champlain.
- **Montmorency Falls Bike Tour:** This tour takes you to the impressive Montmorency Falls, including a ride on the cable car and a walk across the suspension bridge.

Montreal:

Montreal boasts an extensive network of bike paths and is recognized as a bike-friendly city.

1. Lachine Canal Path: A 14.5 km path offering scenic views of the canal and downtown Montreal. It's perfect for a leisurely ride with plenty of stops for picnics and sightseeing.

2. Route Verte: Montreal's section of this extensive network provides numerous routes through the city and connects to broader provincial paths, making it ideal for both urban exploration and longer rides.

Bike Rentals:

- **BIXI:** Montreal's public bike-sharing system, available across the city with convenient pickup and drop-off points.

Walking

Walking is one of the best ways to explore Quebec's rich history and beautiful landscapes.

Quebec City:

- **Old Quebec:** A UNESCO World Heritage site, this area is perfect for a walking tour. Highlights include the Château Frontenac, Place Royale, and the Fortifications of Quebec.
- **Plains of Abraham:** This historic park offers scenic walking trails with panoramic views of the St. Lawrence River.

Montreal:

- **Mount Royal Park:** Designed by Frederick Law Olmsted, this park provides numerous walking trails leading to the Kondiaronk Belvedere, offering stunning city views.
- **Old Montreal:** Walk through cobblestone streets, visit the

Notre-Dame Basilica, and enjoy the historic architecture.

E200
CDI
B 173 DAC

Chapter 8: Must-See Attractions

A. Historic Sites

Old Quebec (Vieux-Québec)

How to Visit:

Old Quebec is the heart of Quebec City and can be easily explored on foot. Start your visit at the iconic Château Frontenac, which overlooks the St. Lawrence River. From there, stroll through the cobblestone streets of Place Royale, the site of the first French settlement in North America. Don't miss the charming Petit Champlain District, filled with boutiques and cafes.

History:

Old Quebec is a UNESCO World Heritage site, known for its well-preserved 17th-century architecture and European charm. The area is surrounded by the only remaining fortified city walls in North America north of Mexico, offering a glimpse into the colonial past of Quebec City. Founded in 1608 by Samuel de Champlain, Old Quebec has played a crucial role in the history of Canada.

Cost:

Exploring Old Quebec is free, but certain attractions within the district, such as guided tours of the Château Frontenac or entry to specific museums, may have admission fees ranging from CAD 10-25.

La Citadelle de Québec

How to Visit:

Located on Cap Diamant, La Citadelle offers guided tours that take you through the fortress and the **Musée Royal 22e Régiment**. The site provides spectacular views of Quebec City and the St. Lawrence River.

History:

Built in the early 19th century, La Citadelle is an active military installation and a National Historic Site. It has been a key defensive structure and is home to the Royal 22e

Régiment, the only French-speaking regiment in the Canadian Forces. The site includes the oldest military building in Canada and various historical exhibits.

Cost:

Admission to La Citadelle and the museum is approximately CAD 18 for adults, CAD 16 for seniors, and CAD 6 for children. Guided tours are included in the ticket price.

Notre-Dame de Québec Basilica-Cathedral

How to Visit:

This historic cathedral is located in the heart of Old Quebec and is easily accessible by foot or public transport. Guided tours are available, and attending a mass can provide a unique cultural experience.

History:

Established in 1647, Notre-Dame de Québec is one of the oldest cathedrals in North America. It has been rebuilt several times due to fires and other damages, but it still retains its historic charm with stunning stained glass windows and intricate woodwork. The basilica is a testament to Quebec's deep religious and cultural heritage.

Cost:
Entry to the basilica is free, but donations are appreciated. Guided tours may have a small fee, usually around CAD 5-10.

How to Reach These Sites

By Air:
Fly into Jean Lesage International Airport (YQB), located about 20 minutes from downtown Quebec City. Taxis, Uber, and rental cars are readily available at the airport.

By Train:
VIA Rail offers regular services to Quebec City from Montreal, Toronto, and other major cities. The main station, Gare du Palais, is conveniently located near Old Quebec.

By Car:
Quebec City is well-connected by highways, making it easy to reach by car. Parking is available throughout the city, including near major attractions.

By Public Transport:
Quebec City's RTC (Réseau de Transport de la Capitale) provides comprehensive bus services

that connect all major attractions. Buses are frequent and reliable, making it easy to navigate the city without a car.

B. Museums and Galleries

Musée de la Civilisation

How to Visit:

Located in Old Quebec, the Musée de la Civilisation is easily accessible by public transport or a short walk from many central hotels. It's a perfect spot for families, history buffs, and those interested in cultural exhibitions.

History:

Opened in 1988, this museum explores the history and cultures of Quebec and the world. It focuses on connecting the past with the present through interactive and innovative exhibits.

Cost:

- Adults: CAD 16
- Seniors (65+): CAD 14
- Students (with ID): CAD 10
- Children (12 and under): Free
- Family packages are available at discounted rates.

Highlights:

- **Permanent Exhibitions:** Include "People of Quebec... Then and Now" and "This is Our Story," which provide a deep dive into Quebec's history and Indigenous cultures.
- **Special Exhibitions:** Rotate regularly, offering fresh perspectives and contemporary topics.

Musée national des beaux-arts du Québec (MNBAQ)

How to Visit:

Situated in the Battlefields Park on the Plains of Abraham, MNBAQ is easily reachable by bus or a short drive from downtown Quebec City. The museum complex is spread across four pavilions, each with unique architectural designs.

History:

Founded in 1933, MNBAQ houses over 40,000 works of art, making it one of the largest art collections in Canada. It showcases the evolution of Quebec art from the 17th century to contemporary pieces.

Cost:

- Adults: CAD 20
- Seniors (65+): CAD 18
- Students (with ID): CAD 10
- Children (12 and under): Free
- Discounts are available on Wednesdays from 5 PM to 9 PM.

Highlights:

- **Pierre Lassonde Pavilion:** Known for its modern architecture and housing contemporary art.
- **Jean-Paul Riopelle Collection:** Featuring a monumental fresco and works by this renowned Quebec artist.
- **Temporary Exhibitions:** Often include international artists and thematic displays, such as the 2024 Rembrandt etching exhibition.

Pointe-à-Callière, Montréal Archaeology and History Complex

How to Visit:

Located in Old Montreal, this museum is accessible by public transit or a short walk from many central attractions. It's a must-visit for those interested in archaeology and the historical development of Montreal.

History:

Founded in 1992, the museum is built on the site of Montreal's original settlement. It showcases the city's archaeological treasures and historical artifacts.

Cost:

- Adults: CAD 22
- Seniors (65+): CAD 20
- Students (with ID): CAD 14
- Children (5-12): CAD 8
- Family packages are available.

Highlights:

- **The Fort Ville-Marie and the First Collector Sewer:** Offering a unique underground archaeological experience.
- **Multimedia Show:** An immersive presentation on the history of Montreal.

- **Special Exhibitions:** Include displays on global archaeology and history.

How to Reach These Museums

By Air:
Fly into Jean Lesage International Airport (YQB) for Quebec City attractions or Montreal-Pierre Elliott Trudeau International Airport (YUL) for Montreal sites.

By Train:
VIA Rail provides regular services to both Quebec City and Montreal, with stations located conveniently near downtown areas.

By Public Transport:
Both cities have efficient public transportation systems with buses and metro lines connecting major attractions.

C. Parks and Natural Wonders

Parc national de la Jacques-Cartier

How to Visit:**
Located just 30 minutes from Quebec City, Parc national de la Jacques-Cartier is a natural haven that's easily accessible by car. It's open year-round, making it a perfect destination for both summer and winter activities.

Highlights:

- **Hiking:** The park offers over 100 km of trails, catering to all levels of hikers. The most popular trail is the Les Loups trail, which provides stunning views of the valley.
- **Water Activities:** The Jacques-Cartier River is ideal for canoeing, kayaking, and fishing. There are calm sections for leisurely paddles and rapids for more adventurous activities.

- **Wildlife:** Home to 43 different mammal species and over 170 bird species, the park is a great spot for wildlife observation.

Cost:

- **Daily Access Fee:** CAD 9.25 per adult
- **Activities:** Canoe and kayak rentals start at CAD 35 for half a day.

Montmorency Falls Park (Parc de la Chute-Montmorency)

How to Visit:

Just a 15-minute drive from Old Quebec, Montmorency Falls Park is accessible by car or public transport. The park is open year-round, offering different experiences in each season.

Highlights:

- **Falls:** The main attraction is the 83-meter-high waterfall, which is higher than Niagara Falls.
- **Activities:** Take a cable car ride to the top, walk across the suspension bridge, or hike the surrounding trails. In winter, the park offers ice climbing on the frozen falls.

- **Views:** The park provides various vantage points to experience the falls' power and beauty up close.

Cost:

- **Cable Car:** CAD 14 per adult
- **Entrance Fee:** Free, but activities like the cable car have additional costs.

Forillon National Park

How to Visit:

Located in the Gaspésie region, Forillon National Park is about 1,000 km from Montreal. It's best reached by car, with various accommodation options including campgrounds and rental cabins.

Highlights:

- **Hiking:** Trails range from easy walks to challenging hikes, such as the famous Les Graves trail leading to Land's End.
- **Wildlife:** The park is known for its diverse wildlife, including bears, porcupines, and numerous bird species.
- **Activities:** In addition to hiking, visitors can enjoy kayaking, whale watching, and exploring the park's beaches.

Cost:

- **Daily Access Fee:** CAD 8.90 per adult
- **Camping:** Fees vary depending on the site and season, typically around CAD 25-30 per night.

Mingan Archipelago National Park Reserve

How to Visit:

This park is located about 900 km from Quebec City and is best accessed by boat tours from Havre-Saint-Pierre. The archipelago is known for its unique limestone monoliths and diverse wildlife.

Highlights:

- **Islands:** Explore the islands' trails, featuring lush forests and ancient rock formations. Île Quarry, Île du Fantôme, and Île Niapiskau are particularly notable for their natural beauty.
- **Activities:** Canoeing, hiking, and bird watching are popular activities. The park is also a great spot for spotting whales and other marine life.
- **Unique Features:** The archipelago is a 450 million-year-old geological wonder, with its rugged landscapes and rare plant species.

Cost:

- **Daily Access Fee:** CAD 6.25 per adult
- **Boat Tours:** Prices vary depending on the tour operator and length of the tour.

D. Festivals and Events

Quebec Winter Carnival

- **Dates:** February 2-11, 2024
- **Location:** Various locations in Quebec City
- **Description:** The Quebec Winter Carnival is one of the world's largest winter festivals, featuring a variety of events including night parades, ice sculptures, snow baths, and the iconic Bonhomme Carnaval. Key events include the Ice Canoe Race on the St. Lawrence River, the International Snow Sculpture Competition, and activities at Bonhomme's Ice Palace.

- **Cost:** The Bonhomme effigy tag, which serves as an admission ticket to most events, costs CAD 20 if purchased ahead of time, and CAD 30 from January 15, 2024. Special packages are available for CAD 55.

Festival d'été de Québec

- **Dates:** July 3-13, 2025
- **Location:** Various venues in Quebec City, including the Plains of Abraham
- **Description:** This is Quebec City's premier summer music festival, attracting over a million visitors. It features performances by international and local artists across various genres. The festival transforms Quebec City into a vibrant cultural hub with concerts, street performances, and art installations.
- **Cost:** Festival passes typically start at CAD 100, with day passes and special VIP packages available.

Les Fêtes de la Nouvelle-France (New France Festival)

- **Dates:** Early August
- **Location:** Old Quebec

- **Description:** This historical festival celebrates the heritage of New France with re-enactments, parades, music, and gourmet activities. Visitors can experience life during the 17th and 18th centuries through interactive displays and performances.
- **Cost:** Most events are free, but some activities and guided tours may have a small fee, usually around CAD 10-20.

Montreal International Jazz Festival

- **Dates:** Late June to Early July
- **Location:** Downtown Montreal
- **Description:** The largest jazz festival in the world, featuring over 500 concerts with artists from around the globe performing jazz, blues, and world music. The festival includes both free outdoor shows and ticketed indoor performances.
- **Cost:** Many concerts are free, while ticketed events vary in price, typically ranging from CAD 40-150 depending on the artist and venue.

Quebec City Pride Festival

- **Dates:** August 30 - September 2, 2024

- **Location:** Various locations in Quebec City
- **Description:** This festival celebrates LGBTQ+ rights and culture with a colorful parade, concerts, drag shows, and community events. It also features arts and culture programs, such as exhibitions and film screenings.
- **Cost:** Most events are free, but some special performances and parties may have admission fees ranging from CAD 15-50.

Festibière de Québec (Quebec City Beer Festival)

- **Dates**: Mid-August
- **Location:** Old Port of Quebec City
- **Description:** A paradise for beer lovers, showcasing a wide variety of craft beers from across Quebec. Visitors can enjoy tastings, meet brewers, and participate in beer-related activities. The festival also features food trucks and live music.
- **Cost:** Entry is typically free, but tasting coupons are available for purchase. Prices for tasting packages generally start at CAD 20-40.

Grands Feux Loto-Québec

- **Dates:** August
- **Location:** St. Lawrence River, near the Old Port of Quebec City
- **Description:** This spectacular fireworks festival takes place twice a week in August, lighting up the sky over the St. Lawrence River. Each show is synchronized to music and offers a magical experience for spectators.
- **Cost:** Free to watch from various locations along the riverbanks.

Plein Art Quebec

- **Dates:** Early August
- **Location:** Espace 400e, Old Port of Quebec City
- **Description:** This large craft fair brings together over 120 professional artisans from across Quebec. Visitors can browse and purchase unique handmade items, including jewelry, pottery, and textiles. The fair also features live demonstrations and workshops.
- **Cost:** Free entry, but purchases vary depending on the artisan.

Chapter 9: Outdoor Activities

A. Hiking and Biking

Quebec City is a fantastic destination for outdoor enthusiasts, with numerous opportunities for hiking and biking. Here's a guide to some of the best trails, including costs and other essential details.

Parc de la Chute-Montmorency

Parc de la Chute-Montmorency offers breathtaking views and exciting hiking opportunities. The park features several trails that provide different perspectives of the stunning Montmorency Falls, which are 30 meters higher than Niagara Falls.

- **Location:** 5300 Boulevard Sainte-Anne, Quebec City, QC
- **Cost:** Admission to the park is approximately CAD $8 for adults, CAD $7 for seniors, and free for children under 17. There are additional costs for the cable car (around CAD $14 for a round trip).
- **Highlights:** The most popular trail involves a scenic climb to the top of the falls via a suspension bridge, providing spectacular views of the falls and the surrounding area.
- **Website:** [Parc de la Chute-Montmorency](https://www.sepaq.com/ct/pcm/)

Parc National de la Jacques-Cartier

Located just outside Quebec City, Parc National de la Jacques-Cartier offers a variety of hiking trails that wind through deep valleys and along the Jacques-Cartier River. The park is known for its stunning natural beauty and diverse wildlife.

- **Location:** 103 chemin du Parc-National, Stoneham-et-Tewkesbury, QC

- **Cost:** Admission is CAD $9 per adult, free for children under 17. Parking is included with the entrance fee.
- **Highlights:** The Les Loups trail is particularly popular, offering panoramic views of the valley. The trail is approximately 11 km round trip and is rated as moderate to difficult.
- **Website:** [Parc National de la Jacques-Cartier](https://www.sepaq.com/pq/jac/)

Corridor du Littoral

The Corridor du Littoral is a scenic bike path that runs along the St. Lawrence River, offering beautiful views of the water and access to several parks and attractions.

- **Location:** Starting in the Old Port of Quebec, the path extends for approximately 13 km.
- **Cost:** Free to use.
- **Highlights:** The path is well-maintained and flat, making it suitable for all skill levels. It's a great way to explore the city while enjoying the fresh air and beautiful scenery.

- **Website:** [Corridor du Littoral](https://www.quebecregion.com/en/what-to-do/activities/corridor-du-littoral/)

Véloroute Marie-Hélène Prémont

Named after the Olympic cyclist, the Véloroute Marie-Hélène Prémont offers a mix of challenging and scenic trails suitable for various skill levels. The route circumnavigates Île d'Orléans, providing stunning views of the St. Lawrence River and the island's charming villages.

- **Location:** Île d'Orléans, QC
- **Cost:** Free to use.
- **Highlights:** The route is approximately 67 km long and offers a variety of terrains, from flat roads to more challenging hills. It's an excellent way to experience the island's natural beauty and historical sites.
- **Website:** [Véloroute Marie-Hélène Prémont](https://www.iledorleans.com/veloroute)

Mont-Sainte-Anne

Mont-Sainte-Anne is known primarily as a ski resort, but it also offers excellent hiking and biking trails during the summer months. The resort features trails that cater to different skill levels and provide stunning views of the surrounding landscape.

- **Location:** 2000 Boulevard du Beau-Pré, Beaupré, QC
- **Cost:** Access to the hiking trails is free, but there is a fee for the gondola ride (approximately CAD $20 for a round trip).
- **Highlights:** The resort offers over 42 km of cross-country mountain biking trails and 7 km of downhill trails. The hiking trails range from easy to difficult, making it a great destination for families and adventure seekers alike.
- **Website:** [Mont-Sainte-Anne](https://mont-sainte-anne.com)

B. Winter Sports

Quebec City transforms into a winter wonderland when the snow falls, offering a plethora of activities for winter sports enthusiasts. Whether you're into skiing, snowboarding, ice skating, or other snowy adventures, Quebec City has something for everyone. Here's a guide to some of the best winter sports activities, including costs and other essential details.

Skiing and Snowboarding

Mont-Sainte-Anne

Mont-Sainte-Anne is one of the premier destinations for skiing and snowboarding near Quebec City. The resort offers a variety of trails for all skill levels, along with stunning views of the surrounding landscape.

- **Location:** 2000 Boulevard du Beau-Pré, Beaupré, QC
- **Cost:** Lift tickets range from CAD $60 to $90 per day for adults, with discounts for children, seniors, and multi-day passes.
- **Highlights:** Over 70 trails, including 19 easy, 23 intermediate, and 28 advanced/expert. Night skiing is available on 19 trails.
- **Website:** [Mont-Sainte-Anne](https://mont-sainte-anne.com)

Stoneham Mountain Resort

Stoneham Mountain Resort is another excellent choice for skiing and snowboarding. It is well-known for its night skiing and impressive snow park.

- **Location:** 600 Chemin du Hibou, Stoneham-et-Tewkesbury, QC
- **Cost:** Lift tickets range from CAD $50 to $80 per day for adults, with discounts available for children, seniors, and multi-day passes.
- **Highlights:** 43 trails, with night skiing available on 19 trails. The snow park is one of the largest in Eastern Canada.

- **Website:** [Stoneham Mountain Resort](https://www.ski-stoneham.com)

Ice Skating

Place d'Youville

Place d'Youville offers a charming outdoor skating experience in the heart of Old Quebec. The rink is free to use and provides a magical atmosphere, especially during the evening when the lights illuminate the area.

- **Location:** Place d'Youville, Quebec City, QC
- **Cost:** Free to use; skate rentals are available for approximately CAD $10.
- **Highlights:** The rink is open daily from mid-December to mid-March, weather permitting. It is a popular spot for both locals and tourists.

Plains of Abraham

The Plains of Abraham offers a large outdoor rink with beautiful views of the city and the St. Lawrence River. It's a great spot for a family outing or a romantic skate under the stars.

- **Location:** 835 Avenue Wilfrid-Laurier, Quebec City, QC
- **Cost:** Free to use; skate rentals are available nearby.
- **Highlights:** Open daily during the winter season, with extended hours in the evening. The surrounding park offers additional winter activities like cross-country skiing and snowshoeing.
- **Website:** [Plains of Abraham](https://www.ccbn-nbc.gc.ca/en/activities/)

Snowshoeing and Cross-Country Skiing

Parc National de la Jacques-Cartier

Parc National de la Jacques-Cartier is an excellent destination for snowshoeing and cross-country skiing. The park offers well-maintained trails that meander through beautiful winter landscapes.

- **Location:** 103 chemin du Parc-National, Stoneham-et-Tewkesbury, QC
- **Cost:** Admission is CAD $9 per adult, free for children under 17. Equipment rentals are available.

- **Highlights:** Over 80 km of cross-country skiing trails and 11 km of snowshoeing trails. The park also offers guided tours and educational programs.
- **Website:** [Parc National de la Jacques-Cartier](https://www.sepaq.com/pq/jac/)

Sentier des Caps de Charlevoix

This trail network offers extensive cross-country skiing and snowshoeing opportunities with breathtaking views of the St. Lawrence River and the Charlevoix region.

- **Location:** Saint-Tite-des-Caps, QC
- **Cost:** Trail access fees are approximately CAD $10 per day.
- **Highlights:** 51 km of cross-country skiing trails and 25 km of snowshoeing trails. The area is known for its scenic beauty and well-groomed trails.
- **Website:** [Sentier des Caps de Charlevoix](http://www.sentierdescaps.com)

Dog Sledding

Aventure Inukshuk

Experience the thrill of dog sledding with Aventure Inukshuk, located near Quebec City. This unique activity allows you to explore the winter landscape while being pulled by a team of energetic huskies.

- **Location:** 4500 chemin Saint-Louis, Stoneham-et-Tewkesbury, QC
- **Cost:** Tours range from CAD $75 to $150 per person, depending on the length and type of tour.
- **Highlights:** Tours vary from short introductory rides to longer excursions. Professional guides ensure a safe and memorable experience.
- **Website:** [Aventure Inukshuk](https://www.aventureinukshuk.com)

C. Water Activities

Quebec City is not only a winter wonderland but also a great destination for water activities during the warmer months. From kayaking and canoeing to whale watching and boat tours, there's plenty to enjoy on and around the water. Here's a guide to some of the best water activities, including costs and essential details.

Kayaking and Canoeing

Parc de la Jacques-Cartier

Parc de la Jacques-Cartier offers excellent kayaking and canoeing opportunities on the Jacques-Cartier River. The park provides a mix of calm waters and exciting rapids, catering to different skill levels.

- **Location:** 103 chemin du Parc-National, Stoneham-et-Tewkesbury, QC
- **Cost:** Canoe and kayak rentals range from CAD $35 to $55 for half a day, and CAD $55 to $75 for a full day.
- **Highlights:** The river's tranquil sections are perfect for beginners, while more experienced paddlers can enjoy the challenge of the rapids. The park also offers guided tours.

- **Website:** [Parc National de la Jacques-Cartier](https://www.sepaq.com/pq/jac/)

Île d'Orléans

Explore the St. Lawrence River around Île d'Orléans by kayak or canoe. The island provides a peaceful and scenic environment for paddling.

- **Location:** Île d'Orléans, QC
- **Cost:** Rentals range from CAD $25 to $50 per hour, with discounts for longer rentals.
- **Highlights:** The calm waters around the island are ideal for a relaxing day on the water. Enjoy views of the island's charming villages and the surrounding river.
- **Website:** [Île d'Orléans Tourism](https://www.iledorleans.com)

Whale Watching

Tadoussac

Tadoussac, located a few hours from Quebec City, is one of the best places in the world for whale watching. Several tour operators offer boat trips where you can see various species of whales, including belugas, minkes, and humpbacks.

- **Location:** Tadoussac, QC
- **Cost:** Whale watching tours range from CAD $70 to $100 per person, depending on the duration and type of boat.
- **Highlights:** Most tours last between 2 to 3 hours and provide an opportunity to see whales up close in their natural habitat. The best time for whale watching is from May to October.
- **Website:** [Tadoussac Whale Watching](https://www.tadoussac.com)

Boat Tours

Croisières AML

Croisières AML offers various boat tours on the St. Lawrence River, providing unique perspectives of Quebec City and its surroundings. Options range from sightseeing cruises to dinner cruises.

- **Location:** Departures from Quebec City Old Port

- **Cost:** Sightseeing cruises start at around CAD $40 for adults and CAD $20 for children. Dinner cruises are more expensive, typically starting at CAD $100 per person.
- **Highlights:** Enjoy panoramic views of Quebec City, Montmorency Falls, and Île d'Orléans. Dinner cruises include a gourmet meal and live entertainment.
- **Website:** [Croisières AML](https://www.croisieresaml.com)

Excursions Maritimes Québec

This company offers Zodiac boat tours that allow you to get closer to the water and experience a more adventurous ride. Tours include exploring the coastline, viewing Montmorency Falls from the water, and discovering marine life.

- **Location:** Departures from Quebec City Old Port
- **Cost:** Tours range from CAD $50 to $75 per person.
- **Highlights:** Zodiac boats provide a thrilling ride with opportunities to see marine wildlife and get unique views of the city and its surroundings.

- **Website:** [Excursions Maritimes Québec](https://excursionsmaritimesquebec.com)

Fishing

Lac Saint-Charles

Lac Saint-Charles is a popular spot for fishing, offering a tranquil setting just a short drive from Quebec City. The lake is stocked with a variety of fish, including trout and bass.

- **Location:** 433 Rue Delage, Lac-Saint-Charles, QC
- **Cost:** Fishing permits are required and cost around CAD $20 per day. Boat rentals are available for an additional fee.
- **Highlights:** The lake is surrounded by beautiful scenery, making it a great spot for a relaxing day of fishing. Both shore and boat fishing are available.
- **Website:** [Lac Saint-Charles](http://www.pechelacstcharles.com)

D. Wildlife Watching

Quebec City and its surrounding areas are rich in diverse wildlife, making it an excellent destination for nature enthusiasts. From bird watching to spotting larger mammals in their natural habitats, here are some top spots and tips for wildlife watching in and around Quebec City.

Bird Watching

Baie de Beauport

Baie de Beauport is known for its bird watching opportunities, especially during migration seasons. The area attracts a variety of bird species, making it a popular spot for both amateur and experienced bird watchers.

- **Location:** 1 Boulevard Henri-Bourassa, Quebec City, QC

- **Cost:** Free admission
- **Highlights:** The wetlands and shoreline provide habitats for waterfowl, shorebirds, and migratory species. Bring binoculars and a field guide to identify different birds.
- **Website:** [Baie de Beauport](https://www.baiedebeauport.com)

Parc National de la Jacques-Cartier

This national park is a prime location for bird watching, with its diverse ecosystems supporting a wide range of bird species. The park's dense forests, river valleys, and mountainous terrain provide ideal habitats for various birds.

- **Location:** 103 chemin du Parc-National, Stoneham-et-Tewkesbury, QC
- **Cost:** CAD $9 per adult, free for children under 17
- **Highlights:** Look out for birds such as the black-capped chickadee, great blue heron, and various woodpeckers. The park also offers guided bird watching tours.

Website: [Parc National de la Jacques-Cartier](https://www.sepaq.com/pq/jac/)

Larger Wildlife

Parc Omega

Parc Omega, located about two hours from Quebec City, offers a drive-through experience where you can see Canadian animals such as bison, deer, wolves, and bears in their natural habitats. The park is designed to give visitors a close-up look at wildlife while maintaining a safe environment for both animals and people.

- **Location:** 399 QC-323, Montebello, QC
- **Cost:** Admission is approximately CAD $25 for adults, CAD $20 for seniors, and CAD $18 for children.
- **Highlights:** The 12-kilometer drive-through path takes you through different ecosystems where you can observe animals in spacious enclosures. There are also walking trails and a farm area where children can interact with domestic animals.
- **Website:** [Parc Omega](https://www.parcomega.ca)

Parc National des Grands-Jardins

This park is part of the Charlevoix Biosphere Reserve and offers excellent opportunities to see larger wildlife, including moose, caribou, and black bears. The park's varied landscapes, from boreal forest to tundra, provide diverse habitats for these animals.

- **Location:** 25 Boulevard Notre-Dame, Clermont, QC
- **Cost:** CAD $9 per adult, free for children under 17
- **Highlights:** The park offers guided wildlife watching tours and educational programs about the local flora and fauna. Early morning or dusk are the best times to spot wildlife.
- **Website:** [Parc National des Grands-Jardins](https://www.sepaq.com/pq/grj/)

Marine Wildlife

Saguenay–St. Lawrence Marine Park

Located a few hours from Quebec City, the Saguenay–St. Lawrence Marine Park is one of the best places for whale watching. The park is home to a variety of whale species, including belugas, minkes, and humpbacks.

- **Location:** Various departure points, including Tadoussac and Baie-Sainte-Catherine, QC
- **Cost:** Whale watching tours range from CAD $70 to $100 per person.
- **Highlights:** Boat tours provide close-up views of whales in their natural environment. Kayaking tours are also available for a more intimate experience.
- **Website:** [Saguenay–St. Lawrence Marine Park](https://www.pc.gc.ca/en/amnc-nmca/qc/saguenay)

Mingan Archipelago National Park Reserve

This park reserve is known for its unique limestone monoliths and abundant marine wildlife. It's an excellent spot for seeing seabirds, seals, and occasionally whales.

- **Location:** Accessible by boat from Havre-Saint-Pierre, QC

- **Cost:** Park entry is free, but boat tours to the islands range from CAD $30 to $70 per person.
- **Highlights:** The park offers guided tours and educational programs about the marine ecosystem. Bird watching is particularly good in the summer months when migratory birds are present.
- **Website:** [Mingan Archipelago National Park Reserve](https://www.pc.gc.ca/en/pn-np/qc/mingan)

Chapter 10: Food and Drink

A. Traditional Quebecois Cuisine

Quebecois cuisine is a rich mosaic of flavors that reflect the province's history, culture, and geography. Rooted in French culinary traditions and influenced by local ingredients and indigenous practices, the food of Quebec offers a unique and hearty dining experience. Here are some of the most iconic dishes:

Poutine

Poutine is perhaps the most famous Quebecois dish, known internationally. It consists of crispy French fries topped with squeaky cheese curds and smothered in rich gravy. Originating in rural Quebec in the 1950s, poutine has become a beloved comfort food with numerous variations, including versions with pulled pork, smoked meat, and even foie gras.

Tourtière

Tourtière is a savory meat pie traditionally enjoyed during the holiday season. This dish is typically made with minced pork, beef, or veal, and spiced with a blend of cinnamon, cloves, and allspice, encased in a flaky pastry crust. The recipe varies by region, with the Lac-Saint-Jean version known for using game meat and a deeper, more pot-pie-like construction.

Soupe aux Pois (Pea Soup)

Pea soup is a hearty staple in Quebec, often made with yellow peas, ham hock, and vegetables. This dish has its roots in the early French settlers' cuisine and remains a comforting, warming meal, especially during the long Quebec winters. It is commonly served with bread and butter and is a feature of many sugar shack menus.

Pouding Chômeur

Pouding chômeur, translating to "unemployment pudding," is a dessert born out of the Great Depression. It is a simple yet delicious dish made by pouring a hot syrup, often maple syrup, over a cake batter, resulting in a moist, sweet cake with a rich sauce. This dessert reflects Quebec's ability to turn humble ingredients into something delightful.

Smoked Meat

Montreal smoked meat is a delicacy that rivals New York's pastrami. The beef brisket is cured with a blend of spices, smoked, and steamed until tender. It is traditionally served on rye bread with mustard, and some of the best-known places to try it include Schwartz's Deli and Lester's Deli in Montreal.

Maple Syrup Creations

Quebec is the world's largest producer of maple syrup, and this sweet nectar features prominently in many dishes. From the classic maple taffy made by pouring hot syrup onto snow to tarte au sucre (sugar pie) and maple ham, the use of maple syrup in Quebecois cuisine is both diverse and delicious.

B. Top Restaurants in Quebec City

Hello! Here are some of the top restaurants in Quebec City in 2024, including their history, descriptions, locations, and other essential details.

1. Chez Rioux & Pettigrew

History and Description:

Chez Rioux & Pettigrew is located in a historic building that once housed a general store. The restaurant embraces this heritage with a nostalgic dining experience, offering innovative dishes made from local ingredients. The eclectic decor, including vintage items and antiques, adds to its unique charm.

- **Address:** 160 Rue Saint-Paul, Quebec City, QC G1K 3W1

- **How to Get There:** A short walk from the Old Port area. Parking is available nearby.
- **Cost:** Entrees range from CAD $20 to $40.
- **Highlights:** Housemade boudin and seasonal brunch options.
- **Website:** [Chez Rioux & Pettigrew](https://www.chezriouxetpettigrew.com)
- **Opening Hours:** Daily from 5 PM to 10 PM, with brunch on weekends from 10 AM to 2 PM.

2. Clocher Penché

History and Description:

Opened in the early 2000s, Clocher Penché quickly became a staple in the Saint-Roch district. Combining the charm of a Parisian brasserie with modern Quebec cuisine, the restaurant focuses on fresh market fare and an extensive wine selection.

- **Address:** 203 Rue Saint-Joseph E, Quebec City, QC G1K 3B1
- **How to Get There:** Accessible by bus routes that pass through Saint-Joseph Street, with parking available in the area.
- **Cost:** Main dishes range from CAD $25 to $45.
- **Highlights:** Fresh market fare and housemade faisselle.
- **Website:** [Clocher Penché](https://www.clocherpenche.ca)
- **Opening Hours:** Tuesday to Saturday from 11:30 AM to 10 PM.

3. La Buche

History and Description:

La Buche opened with the aim of bringing a traditional sugar shack experience to the city. The rustic decor and cozy atmosphere make it a favorite among locals and tourists alike for traditional Quebecois dishes.

- **Address:** 49 Rue Saint-Louis, Quebec City, QC G1R 3Z2
- **How to Get There:** Easily accessible on foot from Château Frontenac. Limited street parking is available.
- **Cost:** Entrees range from CAD $18 to $35.

- **Highlights:** Pouding chômeur with foie gras and bacon, traditional pea soup.
- **Website:** [La Buche](https://www.labuche.com)
- **Opening Hours:** Daily from 8 AM to 10 PM.

4. Honō Izakaya

History and Description:

Honō Izakaya brings a taste of Japan to Quebec City. Established by a group of friends passionate about Japanese cuisine, the restaurant offers a variety of Japanese tapas and charcoal-grilled dishes in a lively atmosphere.

- **Address:** 366 Rue de la Couronne, Quebec City, QC G1K 6G6
- **How to Get There:** Located in the Lower Town, accessible via public transit with several bus stops nearby.
- **Cost:** Small plates range from CAD $10 to $25.
- **Highlights:** Charcoal-grilled yakitori and Japanese-inspired cocktails.
- **Website:** [Honō Izakaya](https://www.honoizakaya.com)
- **Opening Hours:** Tuesday to Sunday from 5 PM to 11 PM.

5. Laurie Raphaël

History and Description:

Founded by Chef Daniel Vézina in 1991, Laurie Raphaël is a fine-dining institution named after his children. The restaurant is renowned for its innovative use of local, seasonal ingredients and its exquisite tasting menus.

- **Address:** 117 Rue Dalhousie, Quebec City, QC G1K 9C8
- **How to Get There:** Situated near the Old Port, it's a short walk from the city's main attractions with ample parking options.

- **Cost:** Tasting menus range from CAD $85 to $150.
- **Highlights:** Innovative tasting menus that highlight Quebec's terroir.
- **Website:** [Laurie Raphaël](https://www.laurieraphael.com)
- **Opening Hours:** Tuesday to Saturday from 6 PM to 10 PM.

6. L'Echaudé

History and Description:
Since its opening in 1984, L'Echaudé has been a cornerstone of the Old Port's dining scene. The restaurant offers a classic French bistro experience with a focus on local ingredients and a bustling atmosphere.

- **Address:** 73 Rue Sault-au-Matelot, Quebec City, QC G1K 3Y9
- **How to Get There:** Located in the Old Port, easily reachable on foot or by bus.
- **Cost:** Main courses range from CAD $20 to $40.
- **Highlights:** Traditional French dishes with a focus on local ingredients.
- **Website:** [L'Echaudé](https://www.lechaude.com)

- **Opening Hours:** Daily from 11:30 AM to 10 PM.

7. Tanière³

History and Description:
Tanière³ offers a modern fine-dining experience in a unique underground setting. The restaurant focuses on immersive culinary experiences with full-course meals that showcase innovative presentations and local ingredients.

- **Address:** 36 1/2 Rue Saint-Pierre, Quebec City, QC G1K 3Z6
- **How to Get There:** Located in the Old Quebec area, it is a short walk from many central hotels.
- **Cost:** Tasting menus range from CAD $100 to $200.
- **Highlights:** Full-course meals with innovative presentations.
- **Website:** [Tanière³](https://www.restaurant-taniere.ca)
- **Opening Hours:** Wednesday to Sunday from 5:30 PM to 10 PM.

8. Le Saint-Amour

History and Description:
Opened in 1978, Le Saint-Amour is a veteran in Quebec City's gastronomic scene. It provides a refined French dining experience with a focus on modern cuisine that highlights regional ingredients.

- **Address:** 48 Rue Sainte-Ursule, Quebec City, QC G1R 4E2
- **How to Get There:** Close to the city center, accessible by foot or by local transit.
- **Cost:** Main courses range from CAD $35 to $60.
- **Highlights:** Modern French cuisine with regional ingredients.
- **Website:** [Le Saint-Amour](https://www.saint-amour.com)
- **Opening Hours:** Daily from 6 PM to 10 PM.

C. Local Markets and Food Tours

Quebec City's local markets and food tours offer an immersive way to experience the region's rich culinary heritage. From bustling farmers' markets to curated food tours, there are plenty of opportunities to explore and savor the flavors of Quebec. Here are some of the best local markets and food tours in Quebec City.

Local Markets

Marché du Vieux-Port

The Old Port Market is a must-visit for anyone interested in local produce and artisanal products. This indoor market is open year-round and features a wide variety of vendors selling fresh fruits, vegetables, meats, cheeses, baked goods, and more.

- **Location:** 160 Quai Saint-André, Quebec City, QC G1K 3Y2
- **How to Get There:** Located in the Old Port area, it is easily accessible by foot or public transit. Parking is also available nearby.
- **Highlights:** Seasonal produce, local cheeses, maple products, and handmade crafts.
- **Website:** [Marché du Vieux-Port](https://www.quebec-cite.com/en/businesses/shops-services/marches-publics/marche-du-vieux-port)

- **Opening Hours:** Daily from 9 AM to 6 PM.

Marché Jean-Talon

Located a bit further afield, Marché Jean-Talon is one of the largest public markets in North America and a paradise for food lovers. It offers a diverse array of fresh produce, meats, fish, baked goods, and specialty foods.

- **Location:** 7070 Henri-Julien Ave, Montreal, QC H2S 3S3 (A drive from Quebec City, but worth the trip for food enthusiasts)
- **How to Get There:** Accessible by car with ample parking.
- **Highlights:** Extensive selection of fresh produce, ethnic foods, and gourmet products.
- **Website:** [Marché Jean-Talon](https://www.marchespublics-mtl.com/en/marches/jean-talon/)
- **Opening Hours:** Varies seasonally, typically from 7 AM to 6 PM.

Le Grand Marché de Québec

Le Grand Marché de Québec is a modern public market that showcases the best of local and regional products. It features over 100 vendors offering everything from fresh produce to gourmet foods and artisanal products.

- **Location:** 250-M, boulevard Wilfrid-Hamel, Québec, QC G1L 5A7
- **How to Get There:** Easily accessible by public transit, with plenty of parking available.
- **Highlights:** Local produce, meats, seafood, bakery items, and specialty products.
- **Website:** [Le Grand Marché de Québec](https://www.legrandmarchedequebec.com)
- **Opening Hours:** Daily from 9 AM to 6 PM.

Food Tours

Tours Voir Quebec - Food Tour

Tours Voir Quebec offers a variety of walking food tours that take you through the historic streets of Old Quebec. These tours provide a chance to sample local delicacies, meet local artisans, and learn about the city's culinary history.

- **Cost:** Tours typically cost around CAD $60 to $90 per person.
- **Highlights:** Tasting local cheeses, meats, pastries, and maple products; visiting historic sites and learning about Quebec's food culture.
- **Website:** [Tours Voir Quebec](https://www.toursvoirquebec.com/en)
- **Booking Info:** Reservations can be made online. Tours are available in English and French.

Quebec City Food Tours - Old Quebec Walking Tour

This food tour takes you on a culinary journey through Old Quebec, stopping at various eateries and food shops to sample traditional Quebecois cuisine. The tour is led by knowledgeable guides who provide insights into the history and culture of the city's food scene.

- **Cost:** Approximately CAD $75 per person.

- **Highlights:** Sampling poutine, crepes, local craft beers, and sweets.
- **Website:** [Quebec City Food Tours](https://quebecfoodtours.com)
- **Booking Info:** Tours run year-round and can be booked online.

Cicérone Tours - Gourmet Food Tour

Cicérone Tours offers a gourmet food tour that explores the flavors of Quebec City through visits to local markets, restaurants, and specialty shops. The tour includes tastings of various dishes and products, highlighting the city's culinary diversity.

- **Cost:** Around CAD $70 to $100 per person, depending on the tour length and inclusions.
- **Highlights:** Visits to local markets, sampling gourmet foods, meeting local chefs and producers.
- **Website:** [Cicérone Tours](https://www.cicerone.tours/en)
- **Booking Info:** Tours are available in multiple languages and can be booked online.

D. Wineries and Breweries

Quebec City is not only renowned for its rich history and vibrant culinary scene but also for its excellent wineries and breweries. These establishments offer visitors a chance to sample some of the region's finest wines and beers, often produced using local ingredients. Here's a guide to some of the best wineries and breweries around Quebec City, including their history, locations, and what you can expect.

Wineries

Vignoble Isle de Bacchus

History and Description:
Vignoble Isle de Bacchus, located on Île d'Orléans, is one of the most renowned wineries in the region. The vineyard was established in the late 1980s and has since become famous for its high-quality wines, including ice wines, white wines, and reds.

- **Location:** 1335 Chemin Royal, Saint-Pierre, QC G0A 4E0
- **How to Get There:** A short drive from Quebec City, accessible by car with parking available on-site.

- **Cost:** Wine tastings start at around CAD $10, with bottles ranging from CAD $20 to $50.
- **Highlights:** Ice wine, guided vineyard tours, and a charming boutique selling local products.
- **Website:** [Vignoble Isle de Bacchus](https://www.isledebacchus.com)
- **Opening Hours:** Daily from 10 AM to 5 PM.

Vignoble Ste-Pétronille

History and Description:
Situated on Île d'Orléans, Vignoble Ste-Pétronille offers stunning views of Montmorency Falls and the Laurentian Mountains. The winery was founded in the early 2000s and has gained a reputation for its excellent white and sparkling wines.

- **Location:** 8705 Chemin Royal, Sainte-Pétronille, QC G0A 4C0
- **How to Get There:** Easily accessible by car from Quebec City, with ample parking.

- **Cost:** Tasting fees are around CAD $10, with wines priced between CAD $15 and $45 per bottle.
- **Highlights:** Sparkling wines, beautiful vineyard views, and seasonal food pairings.
- **Website:** [Vignoble Ste-Pétronille](https://www.vignoblesp.ca)
- **Opening Hours:** May to October, daily from 10 AM to 6 PM.

Domaine de la Source à Marguerite

History and Description:
Located on Île d'Orléans, Domaine de la Source à Marguerite is a boutique winery known for its intimate setting and handcrafted wines. The vineyard was established in the early 2000s and focuses on sustainable viticulture.

- **Location:** 4185 Chemin Royal, Sainte-Famille, QC G0A 3P0
- **How to Get There:** A scenic drive from Quebec City, with parking available.
- **Cost:** Wine tastings cost around CAD $8, and bottles range from CAD $18 to $35.

- **Highlights:** Personalized tours, wine workshops, and stunning views of the St. Lawrence River.
- **Website:** [Domaine de la Source à Marguerite](https://www.lasourceamarguerite.com)
- **Opening Hours:** May to October, Tuesday to Sunday from 11 AM to 5 PM.

Breweries

La Barberie

History and Description:
Founded in 1997, La Barberie is one of Quebec City's most beloved microbreweries. Known for its creative brews and community-oriented atmosphere, it offers a variety of beers that cater to different tastes.

- **Location:** 310 Rue Saint-Roch, Quebec City, QC G1K 6S2
- **How to Get There:** Located in the Saint-Roch district, accessible by public transit or on foot.
- **Cost:** Pints range from CAD $6 to $8, with tasting flights available.

- **Highlights:** Wide selection of beers, including seasonal and experimental brews, and a large outdoor terrace.
- **Website:** [La Barberie](https://www.labarberie.com)
- **Opening Hours:** Daily from 12 PM to 11 PM.

Microbrasserie de l'Île d'Orléans

History and Description:
Located on Île d'Orléans, this microbrewery offers a range of craft beers made with local ingredients. Established in the mid-2000s, it has become a popular stop for visitors exploring the island.

- **Location:** 2471 Chemin Royal, Saint-Pierre, QC G0A 4E0
- **How to Get There:** A short drive from Quebec City, with ample parking on-site.
- **Cost:** Pints are around CAD $6, with flights and growlers available.
- **Highlights:** Beers with local flavors, brewery tours, and a cozy tasting room.
- **Website:** [Microbrasserie de l'Île d'Orléans](https://www.microorleans.com)

- **Opening Hours:** Daily from 11 AM to 8 PM.

Brasserie Artisanale La Souche

History and Description:
La Souche is a craft brewery known for its innovative beers and rustic atmosphere. Established in 2012, it quickly became a favorite among locals and tourists for its unique brews and warm, inviting pub.

- **Location:** 801 Chemin de la Canardière, Quebec City, QC G1J 2B8
- **How to Get There:** Accessible by public transit, with parking available nearby.
- **Cost:** Pints are typically CAD $6 to $8, with tasting flights offered.
- **Highlights:** Creative craft beers, pub-style food, and a welcoming ambiance.
- **Website:** [La Souche](https://www.lasouche.ca)
- **Opening Hours:** Monday to Wednesday from 3 PM to 11 PM, Thursday to Sunday from 11:30 AM to 11 PM.

Chapter 11: Shopping in Quebec

A. Best Shopping Districts

Quebec City is a treasure trove of shopping experiences, each district offering a unique blend of charm, history, and modernity. Whether you're hunting for high-end fashion, unique local crafts, or delicious gourmet treats, Quebec City has something to delight every shopper. Let's take a stroll through some of the best shopping districts you can explore in 2024.

Quartier Petit Champlain

Nestled in the heart of Old Quebec, Quartier Petit Champlain is a picturesque district that feels like stepping back in time. This area boasts cobblestone streets and 18th-century buildings, creating an enchanting atmosphere perfect for leisurely shopping. Here, you'll find boutiques offering locally-made goods, from exquisite jewelry and handcrafted leather products to stylish clothing and Quebec-themed souvenirs.

- **Location:** Rue du Petit Champlain, Quebec City, QC
- **How to Get There:** Easily accessible via the Old Quebec Funicular, which offers stunning views of the St. Lawrence River.
- **Highlights:** Unique local boutiques, seasonal decorations, especially magical during the winter holiday season.
- **Travel Info:** Most shops are open daily from 10 AM to 6 PM, but hours may vary by store. For more information, visit [Petit Champlain](https://www.quartierpetitchamplain.com).

Rue Saint-Jean

Rue Saint-Jean is a vibrant and eclectic shopping street located within the walls of Old Quebec. This lively area is known for its diverse mix of shops, including the historic

Épicerie J.A. Moisan, the oldest grocery store in North America, which offers a range of fine foods and local products. You'll also find an array of bookstores, music shops, and trendy boutiques.

- **Location:** Rue Saint-Jean, Quebec City, QC
- **How to Get There:** Accessible by bus or a short walk from the city center.
- **Highlights:** Historic grocery store, variety of shops, and numerous cafes for a quick rest and refreshment.
- **Travel Info:** Shops generally open from 10 AM to 9 PM, with some cafes and restaurants open later. For details, check [Rue Saint-Jean](https://www.quebeccite.com/en/shopping).

Place Sainte-Foy

For those seeking high-end fashion and luxury brands, Place Sainte-Foy is the premier destination. This upscale shopping mall features an impressive array of prestigious retailers such as Apple, Michael Kors, and Sephora. It's the perfect spot for a sophisticated shopping experience, offering everything from the latest fashion trends to exclusive beauty products.

- **Location:** 2450 Boulevard Laurier, Quebec City, QC
- **How to Get There:** Located along a major commercial artery, easily accessible by car with ample free parking.
- **Highlights:** High-end fashion boutiques, luxury brands, and a refined shopping environment.
- **Travel Info:** Open Monday to Friday from 10 AM to 9 PM, Saturday from 9:30 AM to 5 PM, and Sunday from 10 AM to 5 PM. Visit [Place Sainte-Foy](https://www.placestefoy.com) for more information.

Les Galeries de la Capitale

Combining shopping with entertainment, Les Galeries de la Capitale is home to Eastern Canada's largest indoor amusement park, making it a favorite destination for families. This expansive mall features a wide variety of stores, from fashion and electronics to specialty shops and a large food court.

- **Location:** 5401 Boulevard des Galeries, Quebec City, QC
- **How to Get There:** Easily accessible by car with plenty of parking; public transport options are also available.
- **Highlights:** Indoor amusement park, diverse shopping options, and a large selection of dining choices.
- **Travel Info:** Open Monday to Friday from 10 AM to 9 PM, Saturday from 9 AM to 5 PM, and Sunday from 10 AM to 5 PM. Check out [Les Galeries de laCapitale](https://www.galeriesdelacapitale.com) for more details.

Saint-Roch District

Saint-Roch is Quebec City's trendy, up-and-coming neighborhood, known for its hip boutiques, artisanal shops, and vibrant cultural scene. This area offers an eclectic mix of contemporary fashion, unique gifts, and local art, making it a must-visit for those looking to discover the cutting-edge of Quebec's creative scene.

- **Location:** Rue Saint-Joseph Est, Quebec City, QC

- **How to Get There:** Easily reachable by public transit and a short walk from downtown Quebec City.
- **Highlights:** Trendy boutiques, artisanal shops, and a lively cultural atmosphere.
- **Travel Info:** Most stores are open from 10 AM to 6 PM, with some staying open later. For more information, visit [Saint-Roch District](https://www.quebeccite.com/en/saint-roch).

B. Local Artisans and Souvenirs

Exploring Quebec City's local artisans and finding unique souvenirs is an enriching experience, offering a chance to bring home a piece of Quebec's vibrant culture and creativity. Here's a guide to some of the best spots to discover local craftsmanship and pick up memorable keepsakes.

Le Grand Marché de Québec

Le Grand Marché de Québec is a must-visit for anyone interested in local foods and artisanal products. This bustling market features a wide range of vendors selling everything from fresh produce and gourmet foods to handmade crafts and specialty items. It's a great place to meet local producers and artisans who are passionate about their work.

- **Location:** 250-M, Boulevard Wilfrid-Hamel, Quebec City, QC
- **How to Get There:** Easily accessible by car with ample parking available. Public transit options are also convenient.
- **Highlights:** Fresh produce, gourmet foods, artisanal crafts, and culinary workshops.
- **Travel Info:** Open daily from 9 AM to 6 PM. Visit [Le Grand Marché de Québec](https://www.legrandmarchedequebec.com) for more details.

Île d'Orléans

Just a short drive from Quebec City, Île d'Orléans is a haven for local artisans and producers. The island is known for its charming scenery and a wide variety of locally made products, including wines, ciders, chocolates, and handcrafted items. Visiting Île d'Orléans provides an opportunity to explore small farms, vineyards, and workshops where you can see artisans at work and purchase their creations directly.

- **Location:** Île d'Orléans, QC
- **How to Get There:** About 15 minutes by car from Quebec City, accessible via Route 368.
- **Highlights:** Local wines and ciders, chocolates, handmade crafts, and scenic views.
- **Travel Info:** Many shops and vineyards are open daily, but hours can vary. For more information, visit [Île d'Orléans Tourism](https://www.iledorleans.com).

Quartier Petit Champlain

Quartier Petit Champlain is not only one of the best shopping districts but also a fantastic place to find unique souvenirs created by Quebec artisans. The boutiques in this area offer a wide range of locally made products, including jewelry, clothing, leather goods, and artwork. Each shop has its own character, and the friendly shopkeepers are often happy to share the stories behind their products.

- **Location:** Rue du Petit Champlain, Quebec City, QC
- **How to Get There:** Accessible by the Old Quebec Funicular or a short walk from the Dufferin Terrace.

- **Highlights:** Unique boutiques, handcrafted goods, seasonal decorations.
- **Travel Info:** Shops are typically open from 10 AM to 6 PM, with extended hours during the holiday season. More details can be found at [Quartier Petit Champlain](https://www.quartierpetitchamplain.com).

Marché du Vieux-Port

Marché du Vieux-Port is another excellent spot to discover local foods and crafts. Located near the Old Port, this market features a variety of vendors selling fresh produce, meats, cheeses, and artisanal products. It's a great place to pick up delicious souvenirs like maple syrup, local wines, and gourmet treats.

- **Location:** 160 Quai Saint-André, Quebec City, QC
- **How to Get There:*I** Located in the Old Port area, accessible by foot or public transit.
- **Highlights:** Fresh produce, gourmet foods, artisanal crafts.
- **Travel Info:** Open daily from 9 AM to 6 PM. For more information, visit [Marché

du
Vieux-Port](https://www.marchedesvieuxport.com).

Boutique de Noël de Québec

For those visiting during the holiday season, Boutique de Noël de Québec offers a magical shopping experience. This Christmas-themed store is open year-round and features a wide array of holiday decorations, ornaments, and gifts, many of which are crafted by local artisans. It's a perfect place to find unique Christmas souvenirs.

- **Location:** 47 Rue De Buade, Quebec City, QC
- **How to Get There:** Located in Old Quebec, easily accessible by foot or public transit.
- **Highlights:** Christmas decorations, ornaments, and gifts.
- **Travel Info:** Open daily from 10 AM to 5 PM. Visit [Boutique de Noël de Québec](https://www.boutiquedenoel.ca) for more details.

C. Markets and Boutiques

Quebec City's markets and boutiques are treasure troves of local flavor, artisan crafts, and unique shopping experiences. Whether you're looking for fresh produce, handmade goods, or one-of-a-kind gifts, the city's markets and boutique shops offer a delightful array of options.

Le Grand Marché de Québec

Le Grand Marché de Québec is the city's premier market, attracting locals and tourists alike with its vibrant atmosphere and diverse offerings. This market is home to over a hundred vendors selling fresh produce, meats, cheeses, baked goods, and handmade crafts. It's the perfect place to sample local delicacies, pick up ingredients for a picnic, or find unique souvenirs.

- **Location:** 250-M, Boulevard Wilfrid-Hamel, Quebec City, QC
- **How to Get There:** The market is easily accessible by car, with ample free parking available. It's also well-served by public transit.

- **Highlights:** Local produce, gourmet foods, artisanal crafts, culinary workshops.
- **Travel Info:** Open daily from 9 AM to 6 PM. For more details, visit [Le Grand Marché de Québec](https://www.legrandmarchedequebec.com).

Marché du Vieux-Port

Marché du Vieux-Port is another fantastic market located near the Old Port. This market has a long history and offers a wide variety of fresh produce, meats, seafood, cheeses, and baked goods. It's an excellent spot to explore local flavors and pick up some gourmet treats.

- **Location:** 160 Quai Saint-André, Quebec City, QC
- **How to Get There:** Conveniently located in the Old Port area, it's accessible by foot or public transit.
- **Highlights:** Fresh produce, meats, seafood, cheeses, baked goods.
- **Travel Info:** Open daily from 9 AM to 6 PM. More information can be found at [Marché du

Vieux-Port](https://www.marchedesvieuxport.com).

Marché Public de Sainte-Foy

From mid-May to early November, the Marché Public de Sainte-Foy becomes a bustling hub of local artisans and farmers. Housed in a charming wood-and-glass pavilion, this market offers a delightful array of fresh fruits, vegetables, flowers, and artisanal products.

- **Location:** Avenue Roland-Beaudin, Quebec City, QC
- **How to Get There:** Located in the Sainte-Foy area, it's easily accessible by car or public transit.
- **Highlights:** Fresh produce, flowers, artisanal crafts.
- **Travel Info:** Open mid-May to early November, with operating hours typically from 9 AM to 5 PM. For more details, visit [Marché Public de Sainte-Foy](https://www.marchepublicsaintefoy.com).

Boutique de Noël de Québec

Open year-round, Boutique de Noël de Québec is a must-visit for anyone who loves Christmas. This charming boutique offers a wide range of holiday decorations, ornaments, and gifts, many of which are handcrafted by local artisans. It's the perfect place to find unique holiday souvenirs.

- **Location:** 47 Rue De Buade, Quebec City, QC
- **How to Get There:** Situated in Old Quebec, it's easily accessible by foot or public transit.
- **Highlights:** Christmas decorations, ornaments, gifts.
- **Travel Info:** Open daily from 10 AM to 5 PM. More information can be found at [Boutique de Noël de Québec](https://www.boutiquedenoel.ca).

Saint-Roch District

Saint-Roch is a trendy district known for its eclectic mix of boutiques, cafes, and cultural spots. This neighborhood is a great place to find contemporary fashion, local art, and unique gifts. The area is also home to numerous cafes and restaurants, making it a perfect spot for a leisurely day of shopping and dining.

- **Location:** Rue Saint-Joseph Est, Quebec City, QC
- **How to Get There:** Easily reachable by public transit and a short walk from downtown Quebec City.
- **Highlights:** Trendy boutiques, artisanal shops, vibrant cultural scene.
- **Travel Info:** Most shops are open from 10 AM to 6 PM, with some staying open later. For more details, visit [Saint-Roch District](https://www.quebeccite.com/en/saint-roch).

Quartier Petit Champlain

Quartier Petit Champlain is one of Quebec City's most picturesque shopping areas, known for its charming cobblestone streets and historic buildings. The boutiques here offer a wide range of local products, including handmade jewelry, clothing, leather goods, and artwork. It's an ideal place to find unique souvenirs and gifts.

- **Location:** Rue du Petit Champlain, Quebec City, QC

- **How to Get There:** Accessible by the Old Quebec Funicular or a short walk from the Dufferin Terrace.
- **Highlights:** Unique boutiques, handcrafted goods, seasonal decorations.
- **Travel Info:** Shops are typically open from 10 AM to 6 PM, with extended hours during the holiday season. More details can be found at [Quartier Petit Champlain](https://www.quartierpetitchamplain.com).

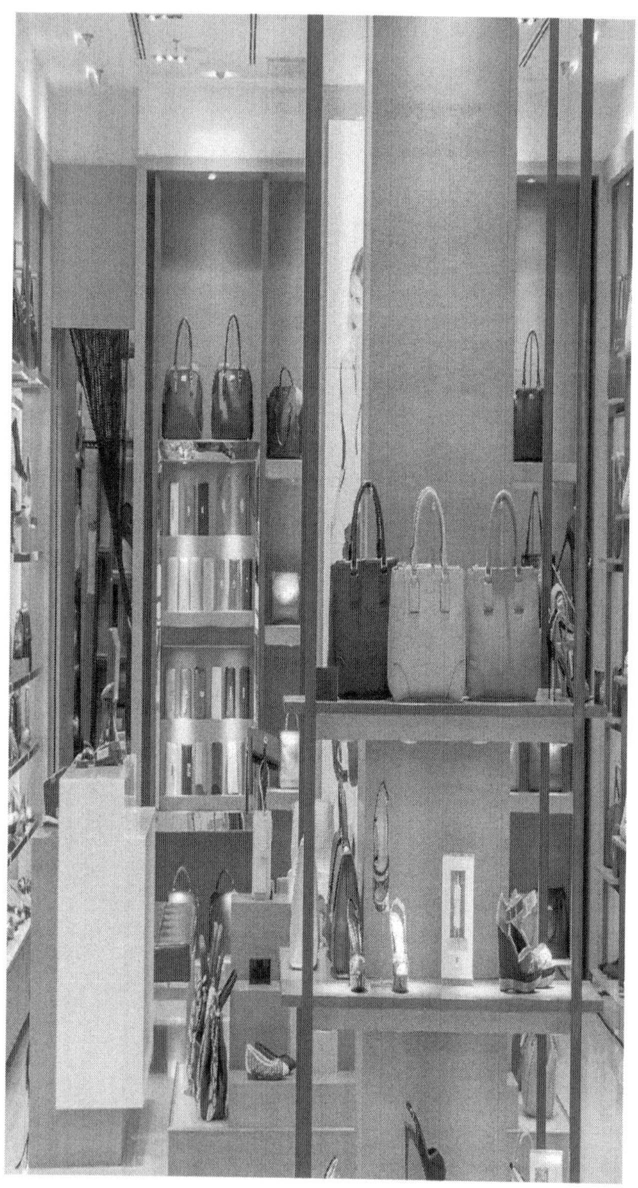

Chapter 12: Cultural Experiences

A. Music and Performing Arts

Quebec City is a vibrant cultural hub, offering a rich tapestry of music and performing arts that captivate both residents and visitors. From grand theaters hosting classical performances to lively festivals and intimate venues showcasing local talent, Quebec City's music and performing arts scene is diverse and dynamic.

Le Grand Théâtre de Québec

Le Grand Théâtre de Québec is the city's premier venue for performing arts, boasting a wide array of events including operas, ballets, symphonies, and theatrical performances. This iconic theater, with its modern architecture and state-of-the-art acoustics, is home to the Orchestre symphonique de Québec and Opéra de Québec, providing a cultural cornerstone for the city.

- **Location:** 269 Boulevard René-Lévesque E, Quebec City, QC
- **How to Get There:** Accessible by public transit and offers parking facilities nearby.
- **Highlights:** The theater hosts a variety of performances throughout the year, from classical music concerts to contemporary dance and drama. Notable events include seasonal symphonies and international opera performances.
- **Travel Info:** For tickets and event schedules, visit [Le Grand Théâtre de Québec](https://www.grandtheatre.qc.ca).

Festival d’été de Québec

The Festival d’été de Québec is one of Canada’s largest and most anticipated music festivals, attracting international and local artists across various genres. Held every July, the festival transforms Quebec City into a bustling hub of musical celebration, with outdoor stages set against the backdrop of the historic city.

- **Location:** Various venues across Quebec City, primarily in the Old Quebec area.
- **How to Get There:** Easily accessible by public transit, with several venues within walking distance of each other.
- **Highlights:** The festival features a diverse lineup of artists, ranging from rock and pop to hip-hop and electronic music. Past performers have included major acts like The Rolling Stones, Lady Gaga, and Kendrick Lamar.
- **Travel Info:** For tickets and the latest lineup, visit [Festival d'été de Québec](https://www.feq.ca).

Palais Montcalm

Known for its exceptional acoustics and intimate atmosphere, Palais Montcalm is a beloved concert hall located in Place D'Youville. This venue hosts a wide variety of musical performances, including classical, jazz, and world music, making it a cultural gem in Quebec City's performing arts landscape.

- **Location:** 995 Place D'Youville, Quebec City, QC
- **How to Get There:** Centrally located and easily accessible by public transit.
- **Highlights:** Regular performances by local and international artists, with a focus on high-quality acoustic experiences. The hall's intimate setting provides a unique and engaging experience for concert-goers.
- **Travel Info:** For tickets and event information, visit [Palais Montcalm](https://www.palaismontcalm.ca).

Théâtre Capitole

Théâtre Capitole, a historic theater built in the early 20th century, is a stunning venue that combines classic architectural beauty with modern entertainment. It hosts a variety of shows, including musicals, comedy acts, and live concerts, making it a versatile and popular spot for both locals and tourists.

- **Location:** 972 Rue Saint-Jean, Quebec City, QC
- **How to Get There:** Easily reachable by foot or public transit, with parking available nearby.
- **Highlights:** The theater's programming includes Broadway-style musicals, stand-up comedy, and concerts by renowned artists. The opulent interior and excellent acoustics make every performance memorable.

Travel Info: For upcoming shows and ticket purchases, visit [Théâtre Capitole](https://www.lecapitole.com).

Impérial Bell

For a more contemporary and edgy experience, Impérial Bell is the go-to venue. This historic venue has been revitalized to host a variety of modern music genres, from indie rock and electronic to hip-hop and punk. Its vibrant atmosphere and eclectic lineup attract a diverse crowd.

- **Location:** 252 Rue Saint-Joseph E, Quebec City, QC

- **How to Get There:** Located in the Saint-Roch district, accessible by public transit.
- **Highlights:** Regular concerts featuring local up-and-coming bands as well as established acts in various genres. The venue also hosts film screenings and special events.
- **Travel Info:** For event listings and ticket information, visit [Impérial Bell](https://www.imperialbell.com).

Les Violons du Roy

Les Violons du Roy is a chamber orchestra renowned for its baroque and classical repertoire, performed with modern vitality and precision. Based in Quebec City, the orchestra regularly performs at the Palais Montcalm and has a reputation for excellence both locally and internationally.

- **Location:** Palais Montcalm, 995 Place D'Youville, Quebec City, QC
- **How to Get There:** Centrally located and accessible by public transit.
- **Highlights:** The orchestra's performances include works by composers like Bach, Handel, and

Mozart, often featuring acclaimed guest soloists and conductors.

- **Travel Info:** For concert schedules and tickets, visit [Les Violons du Roy](https://www.violonsduroy.com).

B. Art and Architecture

Quebec City is a vibrant mosaic of art and architecture, reflecting its rich history and cultural heritage. From stunning historic buildings to contemporary art galleries, the city offers a visual feast for visitors. Here's an exploration of Quebec City's most captivating artistic and architectural sites.

Musée national des beaux-arts du Québec (MNBAQ)

The MNBAQ is a cornerstone of Quebec City's art scene, housing an extensive collection of Quebecois art spanning from the 17th century to the present day. The museum is located in the picturesque Parc des Champs-de-Bataille and features multiple pavilions, each dedicated to different periods and styles of art.

- **Location:** 179 Grande Allée Ouest, Quebec City, QC

- **How to Get There:** Accessible by public transit and offers parking facilities.
- **Highlights:** The museum's collection includes works by renowned Quebec artists like Jean-Paul Riopelle and Alfred Pellan. Temporary exhibitions often showcase international artists, providing a dynamic and diverse artistic experience.
- **Travel Info:** Open Tuesday to Sunday from 10 AM to 5 PM, with extended hours on Wednesdays. For tickets and exhibition details, visit [MNBAQ](https://www.mnbaq.org).

Place Royale and Petit-Champlain

Place Royale is the birthplace of French civilization in North America, featuring beautifully preserved 17th and 18th-century buildings. This historic square is where Samuel de Champlain founded Quebec City in 1608. Adjacent to it is the Petit-Champlain district, known for its charming narrow streets and historic architecture.

- **Location:** Old Quebec, Quebec City, QC

- **How to Get There:** Easily accessible by foot or public transit.
- **Highlights:** Place Royale is home to the Notre-Dame-des-Victoires Church, one of the oldest stone churches in North America. Petit-Champlain is renowned for its boutique shops, art galleries, and cafes, all set within beautifully restored buildings.
- **Travel Info:** Open year-round, free to explore. Guided tours are available for a more in-depth historical experience.

Notre-Dame de Québec Basilica-Cathedral

The Notre-Dame de Québec Basilica-Cathedral is a stunning example of religious architecture, with a history dating back to 1647. It is the mother church of the Roman Catholic Archdiocese of Quebec and has been designated a National Historic Site of Canada.

- **Location:** 16 Rue De Buade, Quebec City, QC
- **How to Get There:** Located in the heart of Old Quebec, easily accessible by foot or public transit.

- **Highlights:** The basilica features a beautiful interior with impressive stained-glass windows, intricate woodwork, and a crypt that houses the remains of bishops and governors. The Holy Door, opened during Jubilee years, is one of only seven in the world.
- **Travel Info:** Open daily for visitors, with services held regularly. For more information, visit [Notre-Dame de Québec](https://www.patrimoine-religieux.com/en).

La Citadelle de Québec

La Citadelle is a star-shaped fortress that is an integral part of Quebec City's fortifications. Built between 1820 and 1850, it is the largest British fortress in North America still occupied by troops. The Citadelle offers a glimpse into military architecture and history.

- **Location:** 1 Côte de la Citadelle, Quebec City, QC
- **How to Get There:** Accessible by foot, located near the Plains of Abraham.
- **Highlights:** Visitors can explore the museum, which showcases the history of the Royal 22e Régiment, and enjoy

guided tours of the fortress. The Changing of the Guard ceremony, held in the summer, is a popular attraction.

- **Travel Info:** Open year-round, with guided tours available. For more details, visit [La Citadelle](https://www.lacitadelle.qc.ca).

Fresque des Québécois

The Fresque des Québécois is an impressive mural located in Old Quebec, depicting significant events and figures from Quebec's history. This large fresco is a remarkable piece of public art that tells the story of the city in a visually engaging way.

- **Location:** 29 Rue Notre-Dame, Quebec City, QC
- **How to Get There:** Located in the Old Port area, accessible by foot or public transit.
- **Highlights:** The mural includes over a dozen historical figures and scenes that reflect the cultural and historical heritage of Quebec City. It is a great spot for photographs and offers an educational insight into the city's past.

- **Travel Info:** Open year-round, free to view.

Parliament Building

The Parliament Building is an architectural jewel of Quebec City, featuring a Second Empire style. It houses the National Assembly of Quebec and is surrounded by beautiful gardens and statues of notable figures in Quebec's history.

- **Location:** 1045 Rue des Parlementaires, Quebec City, QC
- **How to Get There:** Centrally located, easily accessible by public transit.
- **Highlights:** The building's facade is adorned with 26 statues of historical figures. Inside, guided tours offer insights into Quebec's political history and the functioning of its government. The gardens provide a serene spot to relax and admire the architecture.
- **Travel Info:** Open weekdays for guided tours. For more information, visit [Parliament Building](https://www.assnat.qc.ca/en/visiteurs.html).

C. Indigenous Culture and Heritage

Quebec City offers a profound connection to the rich indigenous culture and heritage of the region. Through various museums, cultural sites, and events, visitors can immerse themselves in the traditions, history, and contemporary life of the First Nations. Here's a guide to some of the most enriching indigenous cultural experiences in Quebec City.

Huron-Wendat Museum

The Huron-Wendat Museum, located in Wendake, is a must-visit for those interested in the history and culture of the Huron-Wendat people. The museum showcases artifacts and exhibits that highlight the traditional knowledge, crafts, and history of the Huron-Wendat Nation.

- **Location:** 15 Place de la Rencontre Ekionkiestha', Wendake, QC
- **How to Get There:** Approximately 20 minutes by car from Quebec City.
- **Highlights:** The museum offers guided tours that include visits to a traditional longhouse where you can hear stories and legends told by community members. Visitors can also enjoy

traditional foods like bannock bread and Labrador tea.

- **Travel Info:** Open daily from 9:30 AM to 5 PM. For more details, visit [Huron-Wendat Museum](https://www.tourismewendake.ca/en/musee-huron-wendat).

Onhoüa Chetek8e Traditional Huron Site

This reconstructed Huron-Wendat village offers an immersive experience into the traditional way of life of the Huron-Wendat people. The site features a giant teepee, longhouse, smokehouse, drying racks, and a sweat lodge.

- **Location:** 575 Rue Stanislas-Kosca, Wendake, QC
- **How to Get There:** Easily accessible by car from Quebec City.
- **Highlights:** Guided tours provide insights into the Huron-Wendat way of life, including traditional crafts, transportation methods like snowshoes and canoes, and a traditional meal at NEK8ARRE restaurant.
- **Travel Info:** For more information and booking details, visit [Onhoüa Chetek8e Traditional Huron

Site](https://www.tourismewendake.ca/en/onhoua-chetek8e-traditional-huron-site).

KWE! Meet with Indigenous Peoples

Held annually at Place Jean-Béliveau, KWE! Meet with Indigenous Peoples is a public event that celebrates the cultures, traditions, and contemporary life of Quebec's First Nations and Inuit. The event features artistic performances, culinary tastings, workshops, and much more.

- **Location:** Place Jean-Béliveau, Quebec City, QC
- **How to Get There:** Easily accessible by public transit or car.
- **Highlights:** Experience traditional dances, music, storytelling, and crafts. The event provides an excellent opportunity to learn about the 11 indigenous nations in Quebec.
- **Travel Info:** Typically held in mid-June. Admission is free. For more details, visit [KWE! Meet with Indigenous Peoples](https://www.kwefest.com).

Indigenous Cuisine

Quebec City also offers several restaurants where you can savor traditional indigenous cuisine, which focuses on natural flavors and locally sourced ingredients.

1. La Traite Restaurant

Located within the Hôtel-Musée Premières Nations, La Traite offers a menu featuring local ingredients such as boar, Arctic char, and native plants like wild berries and black spruce.

- **Location:** 5 Place de la Rencontre, Wendake, QC
- **Highlights:** Traditional dishes prepared with a modern twist.
- **Travel Info:** Open daily for lunch and dinner. For reservations, visit [La Traite Restaurant](https://www.hotelpremieresnations.ca/en/restaurant-la-traite).

2. Restaurant Sagamité

Known for its traditional stew made with game meat, corn, squash, and red beans, Restaurant Sagamité provides an authentic dining experience rooted in indigenous culinary traditions.

- **Location:** Multiple locations including Old Quebec and Wendake.
- **Highlights:** Traditional indigenous dishes in a warm, inviting atmosphere.
- **Travel Info:** For more information, visit [Restaurant Sagamité](https://www.sagamite.com).

Chapter 13: Practical Information

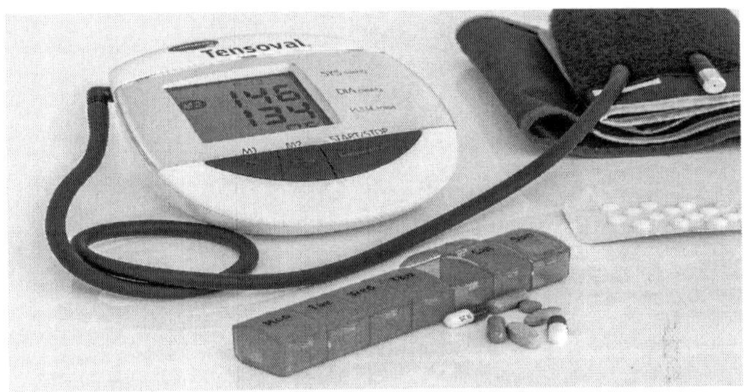

A. Health and Safety Tips

Planning a trip to Quebec City is exciting, but ensuring your health and safety while traveling is paramount. Quebec City is generally safe and has excellent healthcare facilities, but it's always best to be prepared. Here are some essential health and safety tips to help you have a worry-free visit.

Health Tips

Medical Services:
Quebec City boasts excellent healthcare services. If you need medical assistance, the main hospital is Centre Hospitalier de l'Université Laval (CHUL), located at 2705

Boulevard Laurier. For minor ailments and prescriptions, pharmacies are widely available throughout the city.

Routine Vaccinations:

Make sure your routine vaccinations are up-to-date before you travel. There are no specific vaccinations required for traveling to Quebec City, but it's always good to be current with your immunizations.

Travel Insurance:

It's advisable to have travel insurance that covers health, accidents, and theft. This will give you peace of mind knowing that you are covered in case of unexpected health issues or accidents.

Emergency Contacts:

In case of emergencies, dial 911. For non-urgent matters, you can contact the local police at 418-641-6411. Keep these numbers handy during your stay.

Hydration and Diet:

Staying hydrated is crucial, especially if you are visiting during the summer. Quebec City's tap water is safe to drink, so carry a reusable water bottle. Enjoy local cuisine, but be mindful of any dietary restrictions you may have.

Safety Tips

General Safety:

Quebec City is one of the safest cities in Canada. However, as with any tourist destination, be vigilant with your belongings to avoid petty theft. Keep valuables secure and be cautious in crowded areas.

Weather-Related Precautions:

Quebec City experiences a range of weather conditions throughout the year. In winter, sidewalks can be icy. Wear appropriate footwear to prevent slips and falls. In summer, protect yourself from the sun by wearing sunscreen, hats, and sunglasses.

Night Safety:

While Quebec City is safe at night, it's always best to stay in well-lit areas and avoid walking alone in unfamiliar places. Utilize reliable transportation options such as taxis or rideshare services if you are out late.

Natural Disasters:

Quebec City is not prone to natural disasters like earthquakes or hurricanes. However, in winter, heavy snowfall can lead to hazardous conditions. Stay informed about weather forecasts and follow local advisories.

Language Barrier:
While many people in Quebec City speak English, French is the predominant language. Learning a few basic French phrases can be helpful and appreciated by locals.

B. Weather and Packing Guide

Quebec City is a beautiful destination year-round, offering a variety of experiences across its distinct seasons. Preparing for the weather and knowing what to pack can enhance your visit, ensuring you stay comfortable and enjoy all that the city has to offer.

Spring (March to May)

Weather:
Spring in Quebec City sees a gradual warming, with temperatures ranging from 32°F (0°C) to 60°F (15°C). Early spring can still be quite chilly, and there may be occasional snow in March.

Packing Tips:

- **Layers:** Pack a mix of lightweight and warmer layers to adapt to changing temperatures.
- **Waterproof Jacket:** Spring can be wet, so a waterproof jacket is essential.
- **Comfortable Shoes:** Opt for shoes that are suitable for walking and can handle occasional mud or slush.

Summer (June to August)

Weather:

Summers are warm and pleasant, with temperatures ranging from 60°F (15°C) to 82°F (28°C). This is the peak tourist season, with many outdoor activities and festivals.

Packing Tips:

- **Light Clothing:** Bring breathable, light clothing to stay cool.
- **Sun Protection:** Don’t forget sunscreen, sunglasses, and a hat to protect against the sun.
- **Swimwear:** If you plan to visit the beach or enjoy hotel pools, pack your swimwear.

- **Comfortable Sandals:** Ideal for walking around the city and enjoying outdoor activities.

Fall (September to November)

Weather:
Fall brings cooler temperatures, ranging from 32°F (0°C) to 64°F (18°C), and the foliage is spectacular. The air becomes crisp and refreshing, especially in October.

Packing Tips:

- **Warm Layers:** Bring sweaters, long-sleeve shirts, and a warm jacket.
- **Scarf and Gloves:** Early morning and evening temperatures can be quite cool.
- **Sturdy Shoes:** Good walking shoes are essential, as leaves and early frost can make paths slippery.

Winter (December to February)

Weather:
Winters are cold and snowy, with temperatures ranging from 5°F (-15°C) to 30°F (-1°C). Snowfall is frequent, and Quebec City is well-known for its winter festivals and activities.

Packing Tips:

- **Heavy Winter Coat:** A well-insulated coat is a must.
- **Thermal Layers:** Wear thermal underwear, wool sweaters, and warm pants.
- **Winter Accessories:** Hats, gloves, scarves, and insulated boots are essential. Consider packing crampons for icy conditions.
- **Moisturizer and Lip Balm:** Cold air can dry out your skin, so pack moisturizing products.

General Packing Tips

- **Travel Adapter:** If you're traveling from outside North America, bring a power adapter for your electronics.
- **Reusable Water Bottle:** Tap water is safe to drink, and a reusable bottle is eco-friendly.
- **First Aid Kit:** Pack a small kit with basic medications, band-aids, and any personal prescriptions.
- **Backpack:** A small daypack is useful for carrying your essentials while exploring the city.

Weather Resources:

- **The Weather Network:** Check [The Weather Network](https://www.theweathernetwork.com) for up-to-date forecasts.
- **MétéoMedia:** For French-language weather updates, visit [MétéoMedia](https://www.meteomedia.com).

C. Currency and Tipping

Understanding the local currency and tipping customs is essential for a smooth and respectful visit to Quebec City. Here's a detailed guide to help you navigate financial transactions and show appreciation for good service during your stay.

Currency

Local Currency:
The official currency in Quebec City, as in the rest of Canada, is the Canadian Dollar (CAD). The currency symbol is $, and it is often abbreviated as CAD to distinguish it from other dollar-denominated currencies.

Denominations:

- **Coins:** The Canadian currency includes coins of 5 cents (nickel), 10 cents (dime), 25 cents (quarter), 1 dollar (loonie), and 2 dollars (toonie).
- **Banknotes:** The banknotes come in denominations of 5, 10, 20, 50, and 100 dollars.

Exchange Rates:

Exchange rates fluctuate, so it's advisable to check the current rate before your trip. You can exchange currency at banks, exchange kiosks, or through ATMs. Some major establishments might accept US dollars, but it's best to use CAD for better rates and ease.

Credit and Debit Cards:

Credit and debit cards are widely accepted in Quebec City. Visa, MasterCard, and American Express are the most commonly used cards. Contactless payments and chip-and-PIN are standard, making transactions quick and secure.

ATMs:

ATMs are readily available throughout the city, including at airports, banks, and major shopping areas. They offer a convenient way to withdraw Canadian dollars directly from your bank account. Be aware of potential foreign transaction fees.

Tipping

Tipping is customary in Canada and is an important way to show appreciation for good service. Here are some guidelines to help you navigate tipping in Quebec City:

Restaurants:

- It is standard to tip between 15-20% of the total bill before tax. The quality of service can influence the exact amount, but anything less than 15% might be considered a sign of dissatisfaction.
- Some restaurants may include a service charge, especially for large groups. Check your bill before adding a tip.

Bars and Cafes:

- For drinks at a bar, tipping $1-2 per drink is customary. If you're running a tab, a tip of 15-20% of the total is expected.
- In cafes, you can leave a small tip or round up your bill to the nearest dollar.

Hotels:

- **Bellhops:** $1-2 CAD per bag.
- **Housekeeping:** $2-5 CAD per night, left daily or at the end of your stay.
- **Concierge:** $5-10 CAD for exceptional service, such as securing reservations or tickets.

Taxis and Rideshares:

- Tipping 10-15% of the fare is standard. You can round up to the nearest dollar for shorter trips.

Tour Guides:

- For guided tours, it's customary to tip $5-10 CAD per person, depending on the length and quality of the tour.

Other Services:

- **Spa services and hairdressers:** Tipping 15-20% of the total service cost is typical.
- **Delivery services:** For food delivery, a tip of 10-15% or a minimum of $2-5 CAD is appreciated.

Additional Tips

- **Cash Tips:** Tipping in cash is preferred, especially in smaller establishments or for services where the tip might not be processed through a credit card payment.

- **Service Charges:** Always check your bill to see if a service charge has already been included, particularly in restaurants or for group services.

Resources for More Information:

- **XE Currency Converter:** For current exchange rates, visit [XE](https://www.xe.com/currencyconverter/).
- **TripAdvisor Tipping Guide:** For more detailed tipping guidelines, check out [TripAdvisor's tipping guide](https://www.tripadvisor.com/Travel-g153339-s606/Canada:Tipping.And.Etiquette.html).

D. Useful Apps and Websites

Traveling to Quebec City can be greatly enhanced with the help of modern technology. From navigating the city to finding the best restaurants and keeping track of local events, here are some essential apps and websites to make your trip more enjoyable and stress-free.

Travel and Navigation

Google Maps

Google Maps is indispensable for navigation. It provides detailed maps, directions, real-time traffic updates, and information on public transportation. You can also find nearby attractions, restaurants, and hotels with user reviews and photos.

- **Download:** [Google Maps](https://www.google.com/maps)

RTC Nomade

This is the official app for Quebec City's public transit system, Réseau de Transport de la Capitale (RTC). It provides real-time bus schedules, route planning, and service alerts, making it easier to navigate the city by bus.

- **Download:** [RTC Nomade](https://www.rtcquebec.ca/Default.aspx?tabid=95&language=en-US)

Local Information and Services

Bonjour Québec

The official tourism website of Quebec offers comprehensive information about attractions, events, dining, accommodation, and travel tips. It's a great starting point for planning your itinerary.

- **Website:** [Bonjour Québec](https://www.bonjourquebec.com)

Yelp

Yelp is a valuable resource for finding restaurants, cafes, and local services. The app features reviews, ratings, photos, and contact information, helping you choose the best places to eat and shop.

- **Download:** [Yelp](https://www.yelp.com)

Language Assistance

Google Translate

Google Translate is incredibly useful for translating French phrases and menus into English. The app also offers a conversation mode and a camera translation feature, which can translate text from photos instantly.

- **Download:** [Google Translate](https://translate.google.com)

Duolingo

If you want to learn some basic French phrases before or during your trip, Duolingo offers fun and interactive language lessons. It's a great way to familiarize yourself with the local language.

- **Download:** [Duolingo](https://www.duolingo.com)

Weather

The Weather Network

Stay up-to-date with the latest weather forecasts with The Weather Network app. It provides accurate weather updates, alerts, and radar maps to help you plan your activities according to the weather.

- **Download:** [The Weather Network](https://www.theweathernetwork.com)

MétéoMedia

For French-language weather updates, MétéoMedia offers similar services to The Weather Network. It's a popular choice among locals for weather information.

- **Download:** [MétéoMedia](https://www.meteomedia.com)

Events and Tickets

Ticketmaster

Ticketmaster is a reliable platform for booking tickets to concerts, festivals, theater performances, and other events happening in Quebec City. It's convenient for ensuring you don't miss out on any major happenings during your stay.

- **Download:** [Ticketmaster](https://www.ticketmaster.ca)

Eventbrite

Eventbrite is another excellent resource for discovering local events. It lists everything from large festivals to smaller community events and workshops.

- **Download:** [Eventbrite](https://www.eventbrite.com)

Additional Useful Apps

XE Currency Converter

XE is a handy app for converting currencies. It provides up-to-date exchange rates and allows you to set up alerts for specific rate changes, which is particularly useful if you're managing a budget in a foreign currency.

- **Download:** [XE Currency Converter](https://www.xe.com/apps/)

TripAdvisor

TripAdvisor offers reviews, photos, and tips for hotels, restaurants, and attractions. The app is particularly useful for reading detailed reviews from other travelers and getting insider tips on the best things to see and do.

- **Download:** [TripAdvisor](https://www.tripadvisor.com)

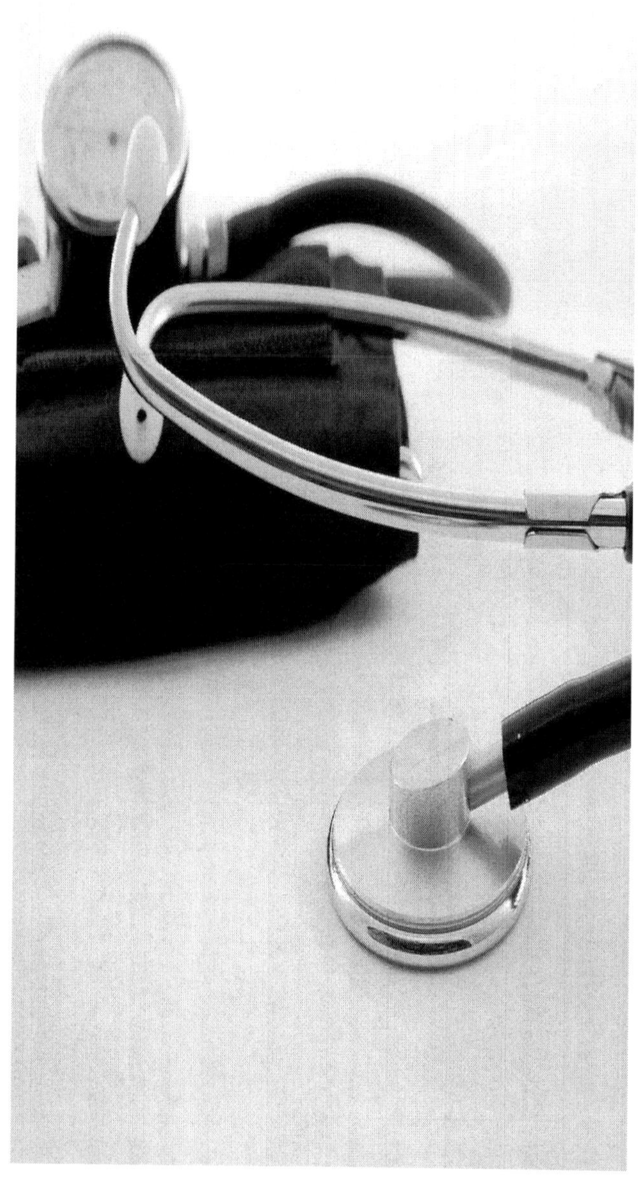

Chapter 14: Quebec with Kids

A. Family-Friendly Activities

Quebec City is a fantastic destination for families, offering a wide range of activities that cater to all ages. From historical sites to interactive museums and outdoor adventures, there's plenty to keep everyone entertained. Here's a guide to some of the best family-friendly activities you can enjoy in Quebec City.

Aquarium du Québec

The Aquarium du Québec is a must-visit for families. This expansive facility is home to over 10,000 marine animals, including fish, reptiles, amphibians, and marine mammals. Kids will love the interactive exhibits and outdoor play areas.

- **Location:** 1675 Avenue des Hôtels, Quebec City, QC
- **How to Get There:** Easily accessible by car with ample parking available. Public transit options are also convenient.
- **Highlights:** The aquarium features polar bears, walruses, and seals, as well as touch pools where children can interact with starfish and other marine creatures. Seasonal events and educational programs make each visit unique.
- **Travel Info:** Open daily from 9 AM to 5 PM. For tickets and more information, visit [Aquarium du Québec](https://www.sepaq.com/ct/paq/).

Parc de la Chute-Montmorency

Parc de la Chute-Montmorency is home to the spectacular Montmorency Falls, which are 30 meters higher than Niagara Falls. This park offers a variety of activities that are perfect for a family day out.

- **Location:** 5300 Boulevard Sainte-Anne, Quebec City, QC
- **How to Get There:** Accessible by car, with parking available. Public transit options include a short bus ride from downtown Quebec City.
- **Highlights:** Families can enjoy the scenic cable car ride to the top of the falls, hike along various trails, and cross the suspension bridge for breathtaking views. In winter, the falls are illuminated, creating a magical experience.
- **Travel Info:** Open year-round, with different activities available depending on the season. For more details, visit [Parc de la Chute-Montmorency](https://www.sepaq.com/ct/pcm/).

Musée de la Civilisation

The Musée de la Civilisation offers interactive and educational exhibits that are fun for all ages. The museum explores various aspects of human history and culture, with a particular focus on Quebec's heritage.

- **Location:** 85 Rue Dalhousie, Quebec City, QC

- **How to Get There:** Located in the Old Port area, easily accessible by foot or public transit.
- **Highlights:** The museum features permanent and temporary exhibits, including hands-on activities and multimedia presentations that engage children and adults alike. Special family programs and workshops are often available.
- **Travel Info:** Open Tuesday to Sunday from 10 AM to 5 PM. For tickets and exhibition details, visit [Musée de la Civilisation](https://www.mcq.org
).

Valcartier Vacation Village

Valcartier Vacation Village is an all-season resort offering a wide range of activities for families. In the summer, it features a massive water park, and in the winter, it transforms into a snow playground with slides and an ice hotel.

- **Location:** 1860 Boulevard Valcartier, Saint-Gabriel-de-Valcartier, QC
- **How to Get There:** About 20 minutes by car from Quebec City, with parking available on-site.

- **Highlights:** The resort includes indoor and outdoor water parks, rafting, go-karting, and an impressive ice hotel in winter. Special events and themed activities keep the excitement going year-round.
- **Travel Info:** Open year-round, with different activities available depending on the season. For more details, visit [Valcartier Vacation Village](https://www.valcartier.com).

Observatoire de la Capitale

For a bird's-eye view of Quebec City, take the family to the Observatoire de la Capitale. This observatory offers panoramic views of the city and beyond, providing a unique perspective on Quebec's landscape.

- **Location:** 1037 De La Chevrotière, Quebec City, QC
- **How to Get There:** Located in the city center, easily accessible by foot or public transit.
- **Highlights:** The observatory includes interactive exhibits that educate visitors about the history and geography of

Quebec City. The 360-degree view is spectacular, especially at sunset.

- **Travel Info:** Open Tuesday to Sunday from 10 AM to 5 PM. For more information, visit [Observatoire de la Capitale](https://www.observatoire-capitale.com).

Plains of Abraham

The Plains of Abraham is a historic site and urban park that offers a wide range of outdoor activities for families. The park is significant for its role in the Battle of Quebec, but today it's a peaceful place for recreation and education.

- **Location:** 835 Avenue Wilfrid-Laurier, Quebec City, QC
- **How to Get There:** Located near downtown Quebec City, accessible by foot or public transit.
- **Highlights:** The park offers walking trails, picnic areas, and historical exhibits. During the winter, it's a popular spot for cross-country skiing and ice skating. The park also hosts concerts and festivals throughout the year.
- **Travel Info:** Open year-round, with different activities available depending

on the season. For more information, visit [Plains of Abraham](https://www.ccbn-nbc.gc.ca).

B. Best Places to Stay with Kids

Here are some of the best places to stay with kids in Quebec City, each offering unique amenities and convenient locations.

Fairmont Le Château Frontenac

The Fairmont Le Château Frontenac is an iconic hotel located in the heart of Old Quebec. Known for its luxurious accommodations and historic charm, it offers numerous amenities that make it ideal for families.

- **Location:** 1 Rue des Carrières, Quebec City, QC

Highlights:

- **Family-Friendly Amenities:** The hotel offers spacious family rooms, an indoor pool, and special kids' packages that include activities and treats.
- **Dining:** Multiple on-site restaurants offer kid-friendly menus.
- **Activities:** The hotel provides guided tours and educational programs about the history of the château.

- **Travel Info:** Check-in from 4 PM, check-out by 12 PM. For reservations and more details, visit [Fairmont Le Château Frontenac](https://www.fairmont.com/frontenac-quebec/).

Hotel du Vieux-Québec

Hotel du Vieux-Québec is a charming boutique hotel situated in the heart of Old Quebec. Its cozy atmosphere and excellent location make it a great choice for families.

- **Location:** 1190 Rue Saint-Jean, Quebec City, QC

Highlights:

- **Family Suites:** The hotel offers spacious family suites with kitchenettes.
- **Complimentary Breakfast:** Enjoy a hearty breakfast included with your stay.
- **Eco-Friendly:** The hotel is eco-conscious, using sustainable practices and offering educational programs on environmental stewardship.
- **Travel Info:** Check-in from 3 PM, check-out by 12 PM. For reservations

and more information, visit [Hotel du Vieux-Québec](https://www.hvq.com).

Hôtel & Suites Le Dauphin Québec

Hôtel & Suites Le Dauphin Québec provides modern accommodations with a range of amenities designed for families. Located a short drive from downtown Quebec City, it's perfect for those looking to explore the city while enjoying comfortable lodgings.

- **Location:** 400 Rue Marais, Quebec City, QC

Highlights:

- **Indoor Pool:** The hotel features an indoor pool with water games that children will love.
- **Spacious Rooms:** Family rooms and suites with extra space for kids to play.
- **Complimentary Breakfast:** A buffet breakfast is included, with a variety of options to start your day.
- **Travel Info:** Check-in from 3 PM, check-out by 12 PM. For reservations and more details, visit [Hôtel & Suites Le Dauphin Québec](https://www.hotelsdauphin.ca/en/quebec).

Hotel Manoir Victoria

Hotel Manoir Victoria is located in the historic district of Old Quebec, offering convenient access to many of the city's attractions. The hotel combines modern amenities with historic charm, making it a favorite among families.

- **Location:** 44 Côte du Palais, Quebec City, QC

Highlights:

- **Family Rooms:** Comfortable family rooms and suites.
- **Indoor Pool and Spa:** Relax and unwind in the hotel's indoor pool and spa.
- **On-Site Dining:** Multiple dining options with kid-friendly menus.
- **Travel Info:** Check-in from 3 PM, check-out by 12 PM. For reservations and more details, visit [Hotel Manoir Victoria](https://www.manoir-victoria.com).

Hôtel Château Laurier Québec

Located just outside the walls of Old Quebec, Hôtel Château Laurier Québec offers comfortable accommodations with a focus on family-friendly amenities.

- **Location:** 1220 Place George-V Ouest, Quebec City, QC

Highlights:

- **Saltwater Pool:** The hotel features a heated indoor saltwater pool.
- **Family Packages:** Special packages for families, including tickets to local attractions.
- **Proximity:** Close to the Plains of Abraham, perfect for outdoor activities with kids.
- **Travel Info:** Check-in from 4 PM, check-out by 12 PM. For reservations and more information, visit [Hôtel Château Laurier Québec](https://www.hotelchateaulaurier.com).

Tips for Booking

- **Advance Reservations:** Family rooms and suites can book up quickly, especially during peak tourist seasons. Make reservations well in advance.
- **Check Amenities:** Ensure the hotel offers amenities that cater to your

family's needs, such as cribs, high chairs, and child-proofing options.

- **Location:** Consider staying in a central location to minimize travel time and maximize convenience for sightseeing and dining.

C. Tips for Traveling with Children

Quebec City, with its family-friendly attractions and hospitable atmosphere, is a great destination for families. Here are some essential tips to ensure a smooth and enjoyable trip with your kids.

Plan Ahead

Book Accommodations in Advance:
Family rooms and suites can fill up quickly, especially during peak tourist seasons. Booking well in advance ensures you get a comfortable and suitable room for your family. Choose hotels that offer family-friendly amenities such as cribs, high chairs, and connecting rooms.

Research Attractions:
Identify family-friendly attractions and activities before you arrive. Make a list of must-see spots and check their operating hours, ticket

prices, and any age restrictions. Websites like [Bonjour Québec](https://www.bonjourquebec.com) and [TripAdvisor](https://www.tripadvisor.com) are great resources for planning.

Create an Itinerary:
Draft a flexible itinerary that includes a mix of activities to keep both kids and adults entertained. Include downtime to allow for rest and spontaneous fun. Over-scheduling can lead to exhaustion and crankiness, so balance busy days with relaxing ones.

Stay Flexible

Allow for Downtime:
Children can easily get overwhelmed by too many activities. Schedule time for naps, quiet play, or simply relaxing at the hotel. This helps them recharge and prevents meltdowns.

Adapt to Changes:
Be prepared to change plans if necessary. Weather, tiredness, or unexpected closures can require a shift in your itinerary. Have a list of backup activities that are indoors or less strenuous.

Involve Kids in Planning:
Let your children help choose some activities. Giving them a say in the planning process can increase their excitement and engagement during the trip.

Pack Wisely

Essential Items:
Pack snacks, water bottles, and a basic first-aid kit. Bring any necessary medications and comfort items such as favorite toys or blankets. Consider packing a small backpack for each child with their essentials.

Weather-Appropriate Clothing:
Check the weather forecast and pack accordingly. Quebec City experiences a range of temperatures throughout the year, so layers are often a good choice. Don't forget hats, sunscreen, and comfortable shoes for walking.

Entertainment for Travel:
Q kids entertained during travel with books, tablets, or travel games. Download movies, educational apps, and games ahead of time to keep them occupied during flights or long car rides.

Use Public Transport

Public Transit System:
Quebec City's public transit system, RTC, is efficient and family-friendly. Buses are a great way to get around, and the RTC Nomade app provides real-time schedules and routes.

Walking and Biking:
Quebec City is very walkable, especially in the Old Quebec area. Consider renting bikes for a fun way to explore the city. Many attractions are within walking distance of each other, making it easy to navigate without a car.

Engage Kids in Learning

Interactive Museums:
Museums like the Musée de la Civilisation offer interactive exhibits that are both fun and educational. Engage children by discussing exhibits and encouraging them to ask questions.

Historical Sites:
Visit historical sites such as La Citadelle and Place Royale to introduce children to Quebec's rich history. Many sites offer guided tours

tailored for families, providing a more engaging experience.

Language Learning:
Encourage children to learn basic French phrases. This can be both educational and practical, as French is the primary language in Quebec City. Apps like Duolingo can make learning fun and interactive.

Safety and Comfort

Stay Hydrated:
Ensure everyone drinks plenty of water, especially during the summer months. Carry reusable water bottles and refill them throughout the day.

Emergency Contacts:
Keep a list of important contact numbers, including local emergency services (911 for emergencies), your hotel, and any local contacts. Teach older children how to use these numbers in case of emergency.

Stay Connected:
Use apps and services to stay connected. Google Maps can help with navigation, while

apps like WhatsApp allow for easy communication with family members.

Chapter 15: Traveler's Resources

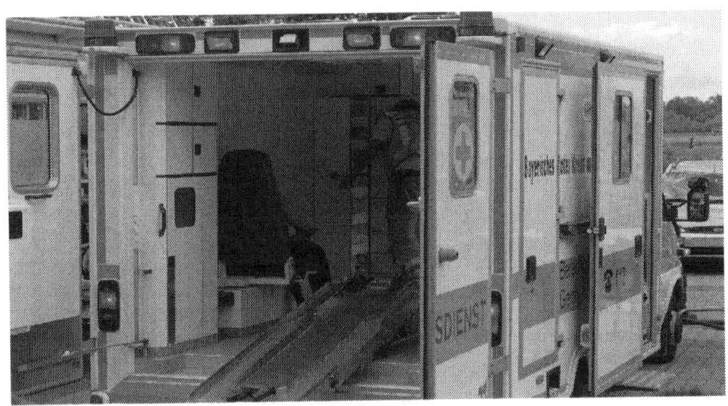

A. Emergency Contacts

When traveling to Quebec City, it's important to be prepared for any emergencies that might arise. Knowing the local emergency contacts can provide peace of mind and ensure you receive prompt assistance if needed. Here are essential emergency contacts and information to keep handy during your visit.

Emergency Services

For immediate assistance in case of police, fire, or medical emergencies, dial 911. This number is universally recognized in Canada and connects you to all emergency services.

Emergency Number: 911

Non-Urgent Police Matters

For non-emergency situations that still require police assistance, such as reporting a theft or lost property, contact the local police department.

Quebec City Police Department: 418-641-6411

- **Location:** Multiple stations throughout the city

Medical Assistance

Quebec City is equipped with excellent medical facilities to handle any health-related emergencies. Here are some key medical centers and hospitals:

Centre Hospitalier de l'Université Laval (CHUL):

- **Address:** 2705 Boulevard Laurier, Quebec City, QC
- **Phone:** 418-654-2151
- **Services:** Comprehensive emergency and specialized medical care

Hôtel-Dieu de Québec:

- **Address:** 11 Côte du Palais, Quebec City, QC
- **Phone:** 418-691-5000
- **Services:** Emergency services and general medical care

Clinique Médicale L'Hêtrière:

- **Address:** 1200 Avenue de Germain-des-Prés, Quebec City, QC
- **Phone:** 418-651-4868
- **Services:** General medical care and walk-in clinic services

Poison Control

For any poisoning incidents, immediate expert advice is available through the Quebec Poison Control Centre.

Quebec Poison Control Centre: 1-800-463-5060

Pharmacies

Pharmacies are widely available throughout Quebec City and can provide medications, health advice, and minor medical supplies. Some major pharmacy chains include:

Jean Coutu Pharmacy:

- **Website:** [Jean Coutu](https://www.jeancoutu.com)
- **Services:** Prescription medications, over-the-counter drugs, health consultations

Pharmaprix:

- **Website:** [Pharmaprix](https://www.pharmaprix.ca)
- **Services:** Prescription medications, health products, wellness advice

Embassy and Consulate Information

If you're an international traveler, it's useful to know the contact details of your country's embassy or consulate in Canada. In case of lost passports, legal issues, or other emergencies, consular services can provide essential assistance.

United States Consulate General:

- **Address:** 2 Rue de la Terrasse-Dufferin, Quebec City, QC

- **Phone:** 418-692-2095
- **Website:** [US Consulate Quebec](https://ca.usembassy.gov/embassy-consulates/quebec-city/)

Other Consulates:

- Check your country's embassy website for the nearest consulate details.

Travel Insurance

Having travel insurance is highly recommended. It covers unexpected medical expenses, trip cancellations, and other unforeseen events. Ensure your insurance includes comprehensive health coverage and keep your policy details and emergency contact numbers handy.

B. Tourist Information Centers

Quebec City is a vibrant destination filled with historical sites, cultural experiences, and modern attractions. To make the most of your visit, it's beneficial to stop by a tourist information center. These centers provide valuable resources, including maps, brochures, event information, and personalized recommendations. Here are some key tourist information centers in Quebec City:

Main Tourist Information Center

The main tourist information center in Quebec City is centrally located and offers a wide range of services to help visitors plan their stay.

Location: 12 Rue Sainte-Anne, Quebec City, QC
Services:

- Maps and brochures
- Information on local attractions, events, and accommodations
- Personalized travel advice
- Guided tour bookings
- Public transportation information

Hours of Operation: Generally open daily from 9 AM to 5 PM, with extended hours during peak tourist seasons.
Contact: 1-877-783-1608
Website: [Quebec City Tourism](https://www.quebec-cite.com/en)

Old Quebec Tourist Information Center

Situated in the historic district, this center is perfect for tourists exploring Old Quebec. It provides comprehensive visitor services tailored to the area's rich history and numerous attractions.

Location: 835 Avenue Honoré-Mercier, Quebec City, QC
Services:

- Detailed maps and guides to Old Quebec
- Information on historical sites, museums, and cultural events
- Assistance with booking guided tours
- Recommendations for local dining and shopping

Hours of Operation: Open daily, with hours varying by season. Typically 9 AM to 6 PM during summer and reduced hours in winter.
Contact: Part of the main tourist information network.

Quebec City Jean Lesage International Airport Information Desk

For travelers arriving by air, the airport's information desk offers immediate assistance to help you get oriented upon arrival.

Location: Quebec City Jean Lesage International Airport (YQB)

Services:

- Maps and brochures
- Information on transportation options to the city
- Assistance with hotel bookings
- Tips on local attractions and events

Hours of Operation: Open daily to coincide with flight schedules.
Contact: Located in the arrivals area of the airport.

Additional Resources

Bonjour Québec - Official Tourism Website: This comprehensive website provides extensive information about Quebec City and the entire province. It includes details on attractions, events, accommodations, dining, and travel tips.

- **Website:** [Bonjour Québec](https://www.bonjourquebec.com)

Visit Quebec City - Official Tourism Website:
Another excellent resource offering guides, itineraries, and practical information for travelers.

- **Website:** [Visit Quebec City](https://www.quebec-cite.com/en)

TripAdvisor:
A valuable tool for finding reviews and recommendations from fellow travelers, covering hotels, restaurants, attractions, and more.

- **Website:** [TripAdvisor](https://www.tripadvisor.com)

C. Language Guide and Common French Phrases

When visiting Quebec City, understanding some basic French can greatly enhance your experience and help you connect with locals. While many people speak English, French is the predominant language. Here's a guide to essential French phrases, their English meanings, and how to pronounce them.

Greetings and Politeness

- **Bonjour** (bohn-zhoor): Hello
- **Au revoir** (oh ruh-vwahr): Goodbye
- **S'il vous plaît** (seel voo pleh): Please
- **Merci** (mehr-see): Thank you
- **Oui** (wee): Yes

- **Non** (nohn): No
- **Excusez-moi** (ehk-skew-zay mwah): Excuse me
- **De rien** (duh ryen): You're welcome
- **Bon matin** (bohn mah-tan): Good morning
- **Bonsoir** (bohn-swahr): Good evening
- **Bonne nuit** (bohn nwee): Good night
- **Enchanté** (ahn-shahn-tay): Nice to meet you
- **Pardon** (par-dohn): Sorry/Pardon

Basic Conversations

- **Comment ça va?** (koh-mohn sah vah?): How are you?
- **Ça va bien, merci** (sah vah byan, mehr-see): I'm fine, thank you
- **Comment vous appelez-vous?** (koh-mohn voo ah-peh-lay voo?): What is your name?
- **Je m'appelle...** (zhuh mah-pell...): My name is...
- **Parlez-vous anglais?** (par-lay voo ahn-glay?): Do you speak English?
- **Je ne comprends pas** (zhuh nuh kohn-prahnd pah): I don't understand
- **Pouvez-vous m'aider?** (poo-vay voo meh-day?): Can you help me?

- **Je suis désolé(e)** (zhuh swee day-zoh-lay): I'm sorry

Directions

- **Où est...?** (oo eh...?): Where is...?
- **À gauche** (ah gohsh): Left
- **À droite** (ah drwaht): Right
- **Tout droit** (too drwah): Straight ahead
- **Près de** (pray duh): Near
- **Loin de** (lwahn duh): Far from
- **À côté de** (ah koh-tay duh): Next to
- **En face de** (ahn fahss duh): In front of

Eating Out

- **Une table pour [nombre], s'il vous plaît** (oon tah-bluh poor [nohmb], seel voo pleh): A table for [number], please
- **Le menu, s'il vous plaît** (luh meh-noo, seel voo pleh): The menu, please
- **L'addition, s'il vous plaît** (lah-dee-syohn, seel voo pleh): The bill, please
- **Qu'est-ce que vous recommandez?** (kes-kuh voo roh-koh-mahn-day?): What do you recommend?

- **Je suis végétarien(ne)** (zhuh swee vay-zhay-tah-ryen / vay-zhay-tah-ryenn): I am vegetarian
- **Sans gluten** (sahn gloo-ten): Gluten-free
- **De l'eau, s'il vous plaît** (duh loh, seel voo pleh): Water, please

Shopping

- **Combien ça coûte?** (kohm-byen sah koot?): How much does this cost?
- **Je voudrais acheter...** (zhuh voo-dray ah-shteh): I would like to buy...
- **Avez-vous... ?** (ah-vay voo...?): Do you have...?
- **Où puis-je trouver...?** (oo pwee zhuh troo-vay...?): Where can I find...?
- **C'est trop cher** (say troh shair): It's too expensive
- **Puis-je payer avec une carte de crédit?** (pwee zhuh pay-ay ah-vek oon kart duh kray-dee?): Can I pay with a credit card?

Health and Emergencies

- **J'ai besoin d'un docteur** (zh-ay buh-swahn dun dok-tur): I need a doctor

- **Appelez une ambulance** (ah-peh-lay oon ahm-byoo-lahns): Call an ambulance
- **Où est l'hôpital?** (oo eh loh-pee-tal?): Where is the hospital?
- **J'ai une allergie à...** (zh-ay oon ah-lair-zhee ah...): I am allergic to...
- **Je ne me sens pas bien** (zhuh nuh muh sahn pah byen): I don’t feel well
- **Avez-vous des médicaments pour...?** (ah-vay voo day may-dee-kah-mahn poor...?): Do you have medicine for...?

Conclusion

Congratulations! By choosing the Quebec Travel Guide 2024, you've taken the first step towards an extraordinary adventure in one of Canada's most captivating provinces. Whether you're dreaming of exploring the charming streets of Old Quebec, experiencing the vibrant culture and festivals, or discovering the breathtaking landscapes, Quebec promises an unforgettable journey.

This guide has equipped you with the knowledge and tools to plan your perfect Quebec escape. You've learned about the diverse regions, the must-see attractions, and the hidden gems that await your discovery. You've gained insights into the rich history and culture of Quebec's people, as well as the modern-day vibrancy that defines this unique province.

With this guide in hand, you can confidently create an itinerary that matches your interests, budget, and travel style. Whether you're a history buff eager to delve into the past, a foodie ready to savor culinary delights, or an outdoor enthusiast seeking adventure, Quebec has something to offer everyone.

As you embark on your journey, may you embrace the spirit of discovery that defines this land. May you marvel at the stunning architecture, immerse yourself in the lively arts scene, and connect with the warm and welcoming people of Quebec.

May your travels be filled with joy, discovery, and wonder. May you return home with memories that will last a lifetime, and a newfound appreciation for the charm and beauty of Quebec.

Safe travels!

We Have a Request from You

Dear Adventurer,

Thank you for embarking on your Quebec journey with the **Quebec Travel Guide 2024**. We sincerely hope this guide has equipped you with the knowledge and inspiration to create an unforgettable experience in this beautiful province.

We would be deeply grateful if you could share your honest review of this guide. Your feedback is invaluable in helping us refine and enhance future editions, ensuring that fellow travelers have the best possible resource for exploring the wonders of Quebec.

Thank you for your time, your insights, and for choosing us as your travel companion.

Safe travels and happy exploring!

[**Albert N. Allred**]

Made in the USA
Middletown, DE
18 August 2024